GOD'S GRACE GOT A HOLD ON ME

THOMAS L. DOBBINS

ISBN 979-8-89130-618-9 (paperback)
ISBN 979-8-89130-619-6 (digital)

Christian Faith Publishing
832 Park Avenue
Meadville, PA 16335
www.christianfaithpublishing.com

Printed in the United States of America

*To our Father Jehovah God and our Lord
and Savior, Jesus Christ (Yahshuah)*

Contents

Acknowledgments

GOD; JESUS CHRIST; my father, John B. Dobbins; my mother, Clara L. Dobbins; my grandmother Louise Dobyne; my granddaddy Oliver Dobyne; my brothers, Grady T. Young and James E. Young; my sister, Patricia A. Dobbins; my step-sister, Deborah Russ; my grandmother Bessie Dobbins; my grandfather Trula Dobbins; my kids—Thomas J. Dobbins, Matthew E. Dobbins, Latricia K. Dobbins, and Rasha J. Hardwick; my pastors—Uncle Brown, my grandmother Louise Dobyne, Pastor E. Shadrach and his wife (first lady Blandy Deline), my cousin Evangelist Lagrant (and her daughter Evangelist Virginia Desmuke and her husband Pastor Carl Desmuke); all the other men and women of God that God placed on my path; and my current pastor Rickey Sanders, thank you all for the love of God that runs deep in me. God bless you. I love you all eternally.

To all my relatives and friends, I love you!

The Beginning after Birth

THE WORLD IS designed to tempt humans. A place merely meant to be a trial is adorned with devious temptations and precarious baits at every single step to mislead the followers. Humans fall in the category of the most phenomenal of God's creations. We are at liberty to think, grow, and expand our intellects.

The Lord has consecrated us with His blessings and benediction. In return for these consecrations, we are to worship Him and love Him the way the Lord is to be worshipped. The belief of an individual is tested by the deceiving world, and an individual's faith is shaken to its core. Only then is the true state of one's belief revealed.

> I will enslave you to your enemies in
> a land you do not know, for my anger
> will kindle a fire that will burn against

you. You understand, O Lᴏʀᴅ; remember me and care for me. Avenge me on my persecutors. You are long-suffering. Do not take me away; think of how I suffer reproach for your sake. (Jeremiah 15:14–15)

The Lord promised to reward those with firm belief and those who stood unshaken in the tumultuous storms of disbelief and despairing moments of chaos. Eminent will be those with such faith in God and rewarded in the best possible way. But the Lord, though amorous and pleasing, announced grave punishments to those who falter on the path of believing and trusting the Lord with all their hearts.

If heaven was promised to the loving disciples by God, hell was also warned about. God clearly devised the rules of whose abiding will lead to glory, but deserting will lead to the deepest lows of hell.

Evil is always working, always in search of new ways to distract the disciple and pull him out of the track. It is the strength of a follower's belief to dodge whatever misdemeanor is being instilled into him and stay on track. But evil has its ways of detracting the disciples from the path that leads them to the Lord and makes them go astray.

I, too, was sidetracked from my path and lost the way. It took years to get back to my origin, but it is not lost if it comes at last.

My story begins from the part when I was still a kid. Playing, running around, and doing goofy things were how I used to spend my days. Childhood was the time when no worries and stress lingered; and I, like any other child, was getting the most out of it. Life sometimes takes twisting turns, and the entire plot can be turned upside down. Something likely happened to me and left me in the middle of chaotic storms and unruly times.

I am Thomas Dobbins, and this is my story!

* * * * *

At the location of a picturesque waterfall falling over the Cahaba River lies the small town of Centreville. The town is known for being the seat of Bibb County and surrounded all over by natural beauty. Luscious green verdure is all one can see wherever the eyes wander. Moreover, the beauty of the town is extensively ornamented by the Cahaba River. Along with adornment, it provides an excellent resort for the local public. People come here with their families to have an invigorating time and revitalize themselves with natural heavenliness.

It was this beautiful little town where I grew up in along with my family. It is about when I was two years old, leading a beautiful life along with my grandparents Louise Dobyne and Oliver Dobyne. My parents, Clara L. Dobbins and John Benjamin Dobbins, loved me dearly. As I was the only child of my parents, I received a fair share of love from my parents and grandparents. I was the apple of their eyes. Brought up in a scenic hometown, I enjoyed the loving shade of my guardians, who were ever concerned about my well-being. I dearly loved my grandfather, to whom I was attached the most. I grew up on work on the plantation. My ancestors were Cherokee. They were Black and German Jews who owned that land, and then we cultivated it further.

My mother was previously married to Curly Young and had two boys with him: Grady Thomas Young and James Earl Young. I was born out of wedlock, and my complete name used to be Thomas Lovett Young. But my granddaddy had the county to change it to Thomas Lovett Dobbins. It was easier as I had no birth certificate inscribed on a letter with a seal signed by the doctor. So the name-changing procedure brought no trouble, and I quite conveniently became Thomas Lovett Dobbins.

Life was going great when all of a sudden, our lives turned to a dark path. When I was around two and a half years old, my grandfather died. Our lives turned upside down, wholly turning at an angle of 180 degrees.

Even at that age, I deeply felt the grief. I was shaken to my core when I saw the face of my granddaddy, and his eyes were closed. He was not moving at all. I vividly remember the last time I saw him. He was dressed in formal attire and lay in a huge box that was about his size. I wondered where they had found the box that fitted him perfectly. It was as if it was made solely for him. I saw him and went running toward him. Everybody was crying, and I could not find the reason they were crying so gravely. I ran straight to my granddaddy and called him.

He gave no response.

I called him again.

And I kept calling and calling him. Again and again.

But there still was no response from his side.

I wondered if he was upset with me. But there never existed a moment where he got upset with me. Even if he did, it would last for a second; and the next moment, we would become great friends, like we always used to be. And now he was not answering me at all. I got anxious and looked up at my grandmother. She was silently weeping into her arm. I then looked at my parents; and they, too, were wiping their tears away. My two-year-old mind could not fathom why they were so sad.

The Death of My Granddaddy

The Lord is close to the brokenhearted and
saves those who are crushed in spirit.
—Psalm 34:18

AND LATER I found out that my grandpa was dead. At an age where I did not even know the meaning of death, that was when my granddaddy left me—or, more precisely, was taken from me.

However, even seeing him that motionless could not crush my hopes; every day, I used to wait for him at the evening snacks, reserving his seat at the table, and did not let anyone else take that seat. Even then, no one dared to take place where granddaddy used to sit. It was as if we all were respecting the place he had even when he was not present there physically. Every day, I used to go to his bedroom to see if he had woken up. Every time I woke up, I would wait for his voice to call me to take a sugar candy from him, the one he kept for me on one condition: I woke up without any help from other house members. And I used to wake up every day without taking any assistance from anyone, all by myself, just to make him proud of me and take that one candy that he kept and reserved just for me.

For days, I did not touch my toys or play with anyone. The cartoon show that I loved the most was not appealing to me anymore, the one show that I used to watch while sitting on Grandpa's lap and eating popcorn or chocolates, or sometimes both. Now, without him, the show was meaningless to me. This whole condition worried my parents and grandma.

They had a discussion and one day came to terms with one decision. We all moved to Chicago as the memories of granddaddy were inevitable for all of us. They wanted to change the milieu for them and, most importantly, me.

I, on the other hand, was never in favor of that decision. I still believed that granddaddy was there, and I did not want to leave him at any cost. I believed that even if he was upset with me and hidden from my sight for some time, he would soon come back to meet me. I did not want him to come back looking for me and find me gone. I wanted to be there whenever he decided to come back, and we could play the way we used to.

I revolted against this decision, never agreeing to their decision. I did not want to move and be shifted into another house when we already had one. Nevertheless, no one bothered enough to listen to a two-year-old, and we moved to Chicago.

With passing time, I turned out to be a rebellious kid. I was traumatized; and the pain of losing my childhood best friend, my lovely grandpa, could not be compensated by any means. I remember going to school, but I was totally rebellious at that time. I did not want to go to school, I did not want to eat anything properly, and I did not want to make any friends whatsoever.

Even years later, I could not make peace with the fact that Grandpa had left me and was never going to come back. I spent so many nights crying, calling on the Lord, and begging Him to give me back my grandpa. I used to learn the verses from Bible that I thought could bring him back to me. I cried and prayed and cried and prayed. But nothing turned out to be fruitful; no prayer was heard, and no plea was listened to. This turning down of hopes and prayers resulted in a lot of anger toward God and in my life. It was actually the obsolete confusion and anxiety about life, and I just could not understand what life was and how it worked.

But the first step in accepting the situation was the hardest, and I was not mentally capable of admitting that one. My mind was not in a state to accept the reality that he was gone and that I had to spend the rest of my life without him. It did not make any sense. He was there with me most of the time, and now he was gone, not present there at all, not for a single second.

He used to come into my dreams and call my name. I could hear the echo of his voice inside my head all day long. There was no way I could get over him. There was no way I could move on, and this fact was driving me insane. I was now old enough to understand the meaning of death but still incapable of getting a hold of it.

My behavior started getting rough; and gradually, I came off as a fiery, insolent boy. I did not listen to whatever my parents said to me as I deemed them to be responsible for leaving the house where granddaddy used to live with us.

Not only did we move to Chicago, but also, this fact was inevitable: we traveled a lot. We did travel a lot. I was in the fifth standard when we moved to Alabama for the summer. I had finished school for a semester or a quarter. My mom, my dad, my sister Patricia, and I would always go back home for the summer. In this way, the summertime was spent in Alabama, and my regular days and months at the school were spent in Chicago. My mind was scattered all over.

> For the Spirit God gave us does not
> make us timid, but gives us power, love,
> and self-discipline. (2 Timothy 1:7)

Feeling the Pain

Have I not commanded you? Be strong and courageous.
Do not be afraid; do not be discouraged, for the
LORD your God will be with you wherever you go.
—Joshua 1:9

I WAS FIGHTING and struggling with the scorching pain in my heart that initiated the moment Grandpa left me. No memories were easy to let go of. I could clearly feel all those moments floating inside me, the moments I spent with him. There was no way I was getting over the fact that he had left and was never coming back. The concept of death was very uncool, and I was absolutely not happy with it, let alone at peace with it.

I vividly remember the last meeting I had with Grandpa. My grandfather was sent to jail for seventeen years. He was accused of killing two innocent people in Alabama. He did time there for seventeen years. It was a log I was sitting on near our wood-chopping area when I saw him. The wood-chopping area was around in front of our yard, and I was sitting there idly when I saw him in the bushes. I saw him, and I felt energy roaring in me. The happiness I felt when I saw his face after all this while was infinite. I don't quite remember whether I was sitting there by myself. I just remember that he did not want his wife or sister to see him. He was talking to me through the bushes. It was fun; it just seemed like a hide-and-seek game we played in the house. I talked to him for a good while. I asked him how he was and told him how everybody in the house was. One by one, I took everyone's names and told him how they were doing. Then I told him about the new toys that Mom had bought me. I told him about the paintings I had made this week. I made him promise that when he would visit, I would show him the painting I had made for him.

But he never did. And that was the last time I saw him alive.

I remember jumping all the way home and telling Mom what I had done. It was such a pleasurable feeling for me that Granddaddy met with me and nobody else and that he talked to me and nobody else.

And now, as I was remembering all this, it was spawning so much anger and rage inside me. All of this resulted in a lot of anger inside me. I was merely four years old, and I had so much anger fueled up inside me.

I belonged to a Christian foundation. This Christian foundation was given to me by my grandmother Louise Dobyne. I had a close relationship with her; whatever I learned about Christianity and my religion was all because of her. She was very loving to me, and I obeyed every word she said. She was a wonderful woman, and there was nobody like her.

> He gives strength to the weary and increases the power of the weak. (Isaiah 40:29)

But even she could not handle me when I rebelled. I used to get frustrated and cry, asking questions—questions that a four-year-old could potentially ask God as all of them were directed to God. I used to question Him, "Why did You put me in a world that is so full of anarchy and chaos?" I wanted to know why it had happened to me. Why did Granddaddy leave, and why was he not going to come back ever? Where had he gone, and why could I not go and bring him back? All of this made no sense to me.

I felt the need to see Granddaddy and talk to him. And being unable to do either of these was making me frustrated. I was not in school yet, so all the time I had for myself was spent in rage. And new questions evolved each day.

Spoiled by Nature

AS I GOT older, I used to sneak out and do things that were unapproved—things that were not approved by my family and prohibited by the family rules. This gave a sense of relief to the uproaring rebellious mood swings of mine, which were getting more challenging with each passing day.

I used to cry every time it rained because I could not go outside in it. I do not know why they prohibited it in the house, but this one rule specifically used to me upset me greatly. I had two friends who would take me out into the rain: Barbara Jean Dobbins and Lillie Ruth Dobyne. They both were my lifesavers, and I always looked forward to seeing them.

The church of Alabama that we used to go to was named Good Hope. Probably about a quarter of a mile away, there was this church for Caucasians. As a kid, I used to believe that the Word of God always made me cry. I always used to sit in the front row with my grandma and cry silently. My lips used to pray for Granddaddy while my heart used to spill tears over his loss. My grandma was one of the elders of the church. Her brother, Brown Chism, was a preacher and a pastor, so one could say that they came from a strong religious foundation. And I was brought up in a similar religious environment.

Being the youngest one in the family, I could not understand why every time I heard the Word of God, I cried. It happened every time I heard the Word of God. Even though I was unable to get that feeling, it was like I understood the Word. I understood what God was and His works. I always felt that the Word of God was always out there, and one needed to just listen to it. A lot of the people did not understand why I was crying. Even at times, I, too, could not comprehend what was it that made me cry all the time.

> For the Word of God is alive and active.
> Sharper than any double-edged sword,
> it penetrates even to dividing soul and
> spirit, joints and marrow; it judges the
> thoughts and attitudes of the heart.
> (Hebrews 4:12)

The Christian foundation given to me was quite strong. The beliefs I had in God were resilient and tough. Even though I was angry most of the time, this anger could not shake my religious grounds. My heart always used to search for the meaning of God and how, in many different ways, one can see Him. I used to observe nature and the surroundings, and everything reflected Him. This is how I was connected with God; but still, at the same time, I was struggling inside myself, within myself.

The rage and anger fueling inside me could not faint the firm faith I had, which was instilled in me since the first day I opened my eyes. The negativity was pulling me toward itself with its full force, but the spark of faith and belief in God did not let me succumb to it fully. It always pulled me back when I was falling into the deep, dark pit of hopelessness and futility. I can say I was fortunate enough to be saved in those troubled times.

But all this internal struggle made me a quiet child. I had stopped playing around all the time or doing childish stuff. Instead, I would be seen sitting quietly in the corner of a room, immersed in some deep thoughts. Most of the time, my face bore that bleak, mean look that fended off most of the kids my age.

> Consequently, whoever rebels against
> the authority is rebelling against what
> God has instituted, and those who do
> so will bring judgment on themselves.
> (Romans 13:2)

I vividly remember the time back where I was in kindergarten. My school campus was located on the west side of Chicago. I was four years old at that time. It was the first day of school, and I did not want to go at any cost. It was almost impossible to convince me to do something that I did not want to do. However, my mother always found ways to make me do them.

> Listen, my son, to your father's instruction, and do not forsake your mother's teaching. They are a garland to grace your head and a chain to adorn your neck. (Proverbs 1:8–9)

She had a way of making me believe that everything would be okay at some point or another. If not now, it definitely will be all right another day, but it will not stay the same always. She used to either sing to me or speak strong words to me, specifically convincing words of faith and substantial belief. I always trusted her. I had no other option but to listen to her, but it was not the only case there. I loved listening to her and whatever she had to say to me.

> Love is patient, love is kind. It does not envy, it does not boast, it is not proud. It does not dishonor others, it is not self-seeking, it is not easily angered, and

it keeps no record of wrongs. Love does not delight in evil but rejoices with the truth. It always protects, always trusts, always hopes, always perseveres. (1 Corinthians 13:4–7)

She made me go to school, and she convinced me to go. And I did go—not because I was convinced to go but just because I wanted to listen to her. I loved her and did not have any other way of telling her. I wanted her to know how much I loved her without actually using the words. I hoped she would have understood. She must have because she used to give me that lovely smile when I said yes with a sulky face in the end. I hoped she knew it every time.

Children, obey your parents in the Lord, for this is right. Honor your father and mother—which is the first commandment with a promise—so that it may go well with you and that you may enjoy long life on the Earth. (Ephesians 6:1–3)

Honor your father and your mother so that you may live long in the land the LORD your God is giving you. (Exodus 20:12)

I remember the worst day in school. I was still in kindergarten and had gone there just because Mom had told me to, and I did not want to upset her. We kids were playing in a 6' × 6' sandbox. While we were playing, a little girl threw sand in my eyes. And, boy, did I scream! I was screaming and crying at the top of my lungs. I already was not liking it here, and then that happened. I was out of control, and no teacher or attendant could restrain my rage. Their efforts were, rather, fueling my rage further. They finally had to call my mom to come and pick me up after all their efforts to appease me failed miserably.

> What more could have been done for my vineyard than I have done for it? When I looked for good grapes, why did it yield only bad? Now I will tell you what I am going to do to my vineyard: I will take away its hedge, and it will be destroyed; I will break down its wall, and it will be trampled. I will make it a wasteland, neither pruned nor cultivated, and briers and thorns will grow there. I will command the clouds not to rain on it.
>
> The vineyard of the LORD Almighty is the nation of Israel, and the people of Judah are the vines he delighted

in. And he looked for justice, but saw bloodshed; for righteousness, but heard cries of distress.

Woes and Judgments

Woe to you who add house to house and join field to field till no space is left and you live alone in the land.

The Lord Almighty has declared in my hearing:

Surely the great houses will become desolate; the fine mansions left without occupants. A ten-acre vineyard will produce only a bath of wine; a homer of seed will yield only an ephah of grain.

Woe to those who rise early in the morning to run after their drinks, who stay up late at night till they are inflamed with wine. They have harps and lyres at their banquets, pipes and timbrels and wine, but they have no regard for the deeds of the Lord, no respect for the work of his hands. Therefore my people will go into exile for lack of understanding; those of high rank will die of hunger, and the common people will be parched with thirst.

Therefore Death expands its jaws, opening wide its mouth; into it will descend their nobles and masses with all their brawlers and revelers. So people will be brought low, and everyone humbled, the eyes of the arrogant humbled. But the LORD Almighty will be exalted by his justice, and the holy God will be proved holy by his righteous acts. Then sheep will graze as in their own pasture; lambs will feed among the ruins of the rich. (Isaiah 5:4–17)

Being a mixed breed and light-skinned caused a lot of problems for my sister and me every day. It is painful for me to say that there was this discrimination among people in the same area even at that time too. The kids in the school were aware of this perception as well and imposed whenever and wherever they found a way to imply it. The quarrels and fights were common for me and my sister in school. It had become a part of our everyday routine. I almost daily had a fight in school. Sometimes I fought for myself; other times, I fought for my sister Patricia. This was one of the main reasons I did not like going to school at all.

Keep me as the apple of your eye; hide me in the shadow of your wings from

the wicked who are out to destroy me,
from my mortal enemies who surround
me. They close up their callous hearts,
and their mouths speak with arrogance.
(Psalm 17:8–10)

From the beginning, we were taught about principles like equality and parity. We were told to treat our friends and foes with equal respect and regard. However, here in the school, even at this young age, I found people behaving the exact opposite of what we had been taught.

So do not fear, for I am with you; do not be dismayed, for I am your God. I will strengthen you and help you; I will uphold you with my righteous right hand.
All who rage against you will surely be ashamed and disgraced; those who oppose you will be as nothing and perish. Though you search for your enemies, you will not find them. Those who wage war against you will be as nothing at all. (Isaiah 41:10–12)

Though I was really disheartened by such behavior and could not understand the reason behind it, I always asked my mom why people behaved like this Why did they hurt the feelings of the people who were just like them? What made them think that they were superior to a group of people? Who was telling them these things? Where was this negativity coming from?

A Psalm of David

The LORD is my shepherd. I lack nothing. He makes me lie down in green pastures, he leads me beside quiet waters, He refreshes my soul. He guides me along the right paths for his name's sake. Even though I walk through the darkest valley, I will fear no evil, for you are with me; your rod and your staff, they comfort me.

You prepare a table before me in the presence of my enemies. You anoint my head with oil; my cup overflows. Surely your goodness and love will follow me all the days of my life, and I will dwell in the house of the LORD forever. (Psalm 23)

My mom always told me that we have to take responsibility only despite all the negativity around us.

It is only us that we would be answerable for, and no other human accountability falls on us.

> Be strong and courageous. Do not be afraid or terrified because of them, for the LORD your God goes with you; he will never leave you nor forsake you. (Deuteronomy 31:6)

Infatuation

TIME KEEPS MOVING on as moving forward is in the nature of time. Time keeps flowing like water. Time and water do not stop for anyone. They keep moving forward, making their way out of all places. They wait for none and keep moving ahead at their own pace regardless of where you are. The choice is up to you—whether you move along with them, adjust your pace in accordance with theirs, and start flowing with their flow or stay back behind, adamant about moving forward. Time never stops for your tragedy to pass or waits for you to get back up on your feet. It keeps walking ahead, leaving it up to you whether you hold its arm and get back up or stay on your knees for days.

> Do not lust in your heart after her beauty or let her captivate you with her eyes. (Proverbs 6:25)

By the grace of God, time kept moving ahead. I was getting older, but the injuries stayed there. At the naive age of eight, I was still a shy, scared little boy when I was in third grade. I always had been this nervous and introverted kid in school and had no idea whether I would be confident ever or not. I still used to be that edgy kid who kept wondering about one thing the whole day and night. Why? Why did it happen? Why was I like this? Why did it specifically happen to me? Why were things happening the way they were happening? Why did things turn out to be the way they did? Why was it still bothering me? Why was I not able to move forward?

> The mind governed by the flesh is death, but the mind governed by the Spirit is life and peace. (Romans 8:6)

As I was deeply immersed in the vexing questions still, life took another turn. It was when I was in Lawson Elementary School, situated in West Side, Chicago, in 1971. My school was just three blocks from my apartment. That school was fun for me. I enjoyed the learning methodologies as they kept me busy and my mind occupied.

> You say, "Food for the stomach and the stomach for food, and God will destroy

them both." The body, however, is not meant for sexual immorality but for the Lord, and the Lord for the body. (1 Corinthians 6:13)

The kids in my class used to discuss diverse topics, but I generally used to avoid getting indulged in those conversations. I kept my focus on my studies only.

So I say, walk by the Spirit, and you will not gratify the desires of the flesh. (Galatians 5:16)

Life took a toll on me, and I did not realize it when I fell into that trap. I do not know how I became infatuated with my teacher who taught me in third grade. This was the first time I ever had those feelings; and that, too, for a teacher who taught me in the school.

Flee the evil desires of youth and pursue righteousness, faith, love, and peace, along with those who call on the Lord out of a pure heart. (2 Timothy 2:22)

I found it absurd and appealing at the same time. I did not know how to counter those feelings and had no idea how to make them go away. I just knew that around her, I used to feel special in a way that I felt nowhere else.

> But I tell you that anyone who looks at a woman lustfully has already committed adultery with her in his heart. (Matthew 5:28)

It was a completely different emotion, something that I had not heard being preached about or ever read about. I had never heard terms like *lust* or *sex*, as I recall. Even though I was completely unaware of those feelings (not that it probably would have mattered), it still felt good, and it made me feel good.

In addition to that, it provided me with false hope and the courage to open up and step up for myself. I used to go outside for recess for about an hour each day. I quite vividly remember this one day when all of us kids were lined up for the race. We were about twenty kids or so, and the distance was about thirty yards, enclosed with a metal fence. That metal fence was our finish line, and whoever touched that metal fence first was going to be the winner of the race. Just listening to the announcement made me excited, and I was motivated enough to win that race. I was determined to win that race just to prove to my teacher that I was not just a kid; I could win things too.

> For everything in the world—the lust
> of the flesh, the lust of the eyes, and
> the pride of life—comes not from the
> Father but from the world. (1 John
> 2:16)

My determination was so fierce that once I started running, I did not even stop once. It was as if I could not stop at all and kept on running. The last thing I remember is that I was running, and it all went blank.

Later I woke up in my third-grade classroom, waiting for my parents. I was told that while running, I had knocked myself out on the metal fence and fainted because of an intense blow on my head and an excessive drainage of energy. I had long drawn out my stamina, which resulted in this incident.

Only then did I realize that I could not feel any sensation in my legs. Fear crept inside my brain, making me all fretful and anxious. My mind stopped working once I was told that I was paralyzed from the waist down.

> No, in all these things, we are more than
> conquerors through him who loved us.
> (Romans 8:37)

When my brother James got to know that this had happened to me, he was furious. He carried me home in his arms, his tears running down his face the whole time. When we got close to the house, he burst out all of what he had been keeping inside. He started yelling, telling everyone what had happened to me. He was screaming above his throat, saying, "Who hurt my brother?"

> But each person is tempted when they are dragged away by their own evil desire and enticed. Then, after desire has conceived, it gives birth to sin; and sin, when it is full-grown, gives birth to death. (James 1:14–15)

Paralyzed

THE DOCTOR, AFTER observing my condition, told my parents that the paralysis I was facing was temporary. The damage done to the nerves and muscles was transitory; and with time, the healing would take place, making the paralyzed condition go away. As the doctors projected, it lasted for about a year.

During this whole period, my rage grew stronger. The frustration that had been building up inside me was now getting worse because of the situation. I refused to eat anything laid in front of me. Life had not been any easier for me since day one, and now I was paralyzed! One could imagine the extent of frustration I had been facing in that era of immobility. I could not get out of my house, I could not get out of my room, and I could not get out of my bed, even. If this is not enough to make someone go crazy, then what would? Those moments made me feel like the most miserable human on Earth, and I could do nothing about it. Nobody could. Those moments made me feel the most wretched I have ever felt in my life. It made me miss my grandfather more desolately. In those gloomy moments, I missed him so badly and the house that we had left behind. I was in Chicago, away from my grandfather and my house, and now I could do nothing except lie in my bed and stare at the ceiling. I badly missed my third-grade teacher, and there was no way I could get back to her. What was all this even happening with me? Why was it all happening to me?

I was unable to hear the Word of God in my house. The reason had been that my mother and father were not going to church, and I myself was unable to go there because of the state I was in. Not hearing the Word of God made me anxious as it made me feel that God was unhappy with me and not talking to me. This distance from God created a lot of chaos in my mind and my life.

> Jesus answered, "It is written: Man shall not live on bread alone, but on every word that comes from the mouth of God." (Matthew 4:4)

It was not as if I was getting ignored or overlooked by the people around me. No, my parents and all the relatives showed me a lot of attention and additional affection in that time period, but that frustration was not letting me see anything good. I was irritated and annoyed the whole day, the whole week, and the whole year. Nobody's love and affection could fill the void that I had been feeling inside my soul.

> Carry each other's burdens, and in this
> way, you will fulfill the law of Christ.
> (Galatians 6:2)

And then one day, out of nowhere, something really peculiar happened to me. One night, I had a strange dream. I do not exactly remember the dream, but it was sexual and led me to have my first ever climax. And that, too, in my dream while I was asleep. I woke up all shocked and flustered as to what had happened to me. I was at the age where I did not even know what I had just experienced.

> When tempted, no one should say,
> "God is tempting me." For God cannot
> be tempted by evil, nor does he tempt
> anyone; but each person is tempted
> when they are dragged away by their
> own evil desire and enticed. (James
> 1:13–14)

> But I tell you that anyone who looks
> at a woman lustfully has already com-
> mitted adultery with her in his heart.
> (Matthew 5:28)

My mother and father worked the third shift, so they had to leave home around 12:30 p.m. and return home around midnight. This comprised almost an entire day and was the job shift they performed from Monday until Friday. Therefore, they were not home almost all day. This left my sister and me alone at home. We would be all by ourselves. It generated a need for me to grow up fast and be aware of my responsibilities even before I reached the age where usually a child is handed his or her responsibilities. I had to do it for my sister and myself as there was no other option left. At that time, I was a six-year-old kid, while my sister Patricia was three years old. We had been given a set of rules that included not opening the door for anyone but our parents and staying out of the windows. This was strictly followed until our parents started trusting our neighbors and felt comfortable with them.

> So in everything, do to others what
> you would have them do to you, for
> this sums up the Law and the Prophets.
> (Matthew 7:12)

Even after two years, the condition was the same. Both our parents used to work for the day, but this time it was different. While Mom and Dad worked, we stayed with a neighbor upstairs. It was Ms. Sanders. She was a single mother of seven kids. That included six boys and a girl. There was an extended amount of time that we used to spend with each other. This made us connect deeply, and we became one unit, a family.

> Finally, all of you, be like-minded, be sympathetic, love one another, be compassionate and humble. (1 Peter 3:8)

The bond we shared with one another was the most beautiful one. It was more than friendship and blood relations. Ms. Sanders used to treat us like her own kids, and they were always welcome at our house.

> No one should seek their own good, but the good of others. (1 Corinthians 10:24)

The thing I loved the most about Ms. Sanders was that she always taught her kids about God and gave them the lesson about respecting their elders. During such conversations with her kids, she used to include us too among them as good manners are equally applicable to everyone; that was what she believed. I loved

Ms. Sanders dearly and listened to everything she had to say.

> Love the Lord your God with all your heart and with all your soul and with all your mind and with all your strength. The second is this: "Love your neighbor as yourself." There is no commandment greater than these. (Mark 12:30–31)

The people living in our neighborhood were varied and comprised of Jews and Blacks, the neighborhood of 1241 S Central Park, West Side, Chicago. Everybody was new to one another. Nobody had any idea whom they were living next to. However, people gradually got to know one another, and it became the most peaceful area of all.

> The second is this: "Love your neighbor as yourself." There is no commandment greater than these. (Mark 12:31)

Just next to our apartment, we had a store with a fruit stand. They used to water it every morning. We also had the central park show up the street where

Michael Jackson once performed one of his first live shows.

> For the entire law is fulfilled in keeping this one command: "Love your neighbor as yourself." (Galatians 5:14)

Before Martin Luther King Jr. died, it was a quiet and serene neighborhood, but everything changed with the tragic incident that happened. The day he was assassinated, people were so agitated and enraged that they looted and burned down almost all the stores in our area. The disruption and extremism led the people to abandon the neighborhood. After that the Jews started moving out, and with them leaving, the street gangs moved in.

> Keep on loving one another as brothers and sisters. Do not forget to show hospitality to strangers, for by so doing, some people have shown hospitality to angels without knowing it. (Hebrews 13:1–2)

Something happened then that I could not even think about in my dreams. I could not even perceive it in my darkest of dreams. A lust spirit was conceived in me. And for that, I got baptized when I was at the young age of thirteen with Rickey Sanders, one of Ms. Sanders's sons. The baptizing ceremony took place at Joshua Missionary Baptist Church in Chicago and was officiated by Pastor White. It was the time where I was not going to church regularly just because I needed to fit in with my peers. My parents knew how asocial I was getting, and it obviously was not good for me when I was in the personality-development age. My father ordered me to go sit with my friends and develop some courtship with my classmates. I badly needed it, and my father knew too well that I would not do this on my own. So he demanded me to go, and I could not deny his orders.

> Do not be misled: "Bad company corrupts good character." (1 Corinthians 15:33)

This made the misconception clear of why I had those lustful feelings at such a young age. It was not me. It could never be me. That spirit was making me do all that, and I was just succumbing to it. I was losing control, and it was getting a hold of me. My family and I were really grateful and overwhelmed when it got away from me.

> No temptation has overtaken you except what is common to mankind.

> And God is faithful; he will not let you
> be tempted beyond what you can bear.
> But when you are tempted, he will
> also provide a way out so that you can
> endure it. (1 Corinthians 10:13)

My parents thought going to church would help me out of my depression. They were correct in their own way, but I needed to heal on my own. No matter how hard everyone tries to make you understand something, you learn lessons from your own experiences. My mind had gone rigid, and I was resilient to almost all the counseling coming my way. I quite vividly remember the day where I was in our pantry (I was between the ages of five and six) and climbed up onto the fourth shelf. It was the last shelf, and there I had a debate with God concerning suicide. I was asking God why He had put me in this tormented world.

> The righteous cry out, and the LORD
> hears them; he delivers them from all
> their troubles. The LORD is close to the
> brokenhearted and saves those who are
> crushed in spirit. (Psalm 34:17–18)

I was really exasperated by the incidents happening in my life. It was written all over my face and seen in how my hands were shaking when I talked to God.

I was threatening God to answer right away, or else I would tie a light cord from the ceiling around my neck and jump down. God did not answer. How was God supposed to answer me right at that moment? I really got anxious and prayed that my prayers would get answered. Whenever I saw people like me sitting in the church, crying out to God about their lives, I used to get upset. It saddened me a great deal to see a human being so done with life that he or she was giving up on it and talking about ending it with their own hands. Nothing can sound more heartbreaking than a man who has given up all hope in his life. Even though I was extremely exasperated with my life, I never dared to take such thoughts to a more serious level. Nor did I find the courage to do it. Therefore, although I was really frustrated and tired of my life, I still could not find the nerve to take my life into my own hands.

> But he said to me, "My grace is sufficient for you, for my power is made perfect in weakness." Therefore I will boast all the more gladly about my weaknesses, so that Christ's power may rest on me. (2 Corinthians 12:9)

Alone but Not

THE SUDDEN AND unexpected demise of Martin Luther King Jr. created huge ripples in the calm. The serenity was hugely affected by this shocking incident and affected people at every level in the country. Not only the commercial sector but also the education sector and even all the minor sectors got hit by the thunderstorm that was generated by this happening. It was not only dismaying and upsetting but also shocking for the entire public. He was a hero to many, and a lot of people had great expectations from him. He was doing a lot of things for the welfare of his people, and he had to make a great many amendments and begin worthwhile developmental projects. The public had become so furious that a number of protests and disputes originated and could be seen in almost the entire country.

It would not be wrong to say that whole cities were on fire.

> For the Spirit God gave us does not
> make us timid, but gives us power, love
> and self-discipline. (2 Timothy 1:7)

In addition, most of the time, in such situations, my sister and I would be alone at home. There were moments where my sister and I were alone in the house, and we could often see the whole thing from the windows of our very own house. We were shaken to our core at the instances of streetlight blackouts. Those really were the scariest of times, and I cannot imagine how we as kids managed to cope with it. It was creepy having the entire city block as the blackout of the streetlights just leads to a dark city. Every corner and every nook of the city would become completely obscure, giving away no traces of light. The nights became long, and we did nothing but wait for the sun to rise. The sun became our only hope for a source of luminescence, and no artificial thing was allowed to produce light until it rose up from the east.

> So do not fear, for I am with you; do
> not be dismayed, for I am your God. I
> will strengthen you and help you; I will

uphold you with my righteous right hand. (Isaiah 41:10)

We used to be absolutely anxious until our parents entered our houses. Their safety and well-being kept us awake most of the night. How could we sleep with our parents out of the house, away from the safe place, out in the area where danger prevailed? The entire time, my sister and I would repeat the verses from the Bible that our parents and grandparents taught us. There were many great verses that we had learned and knew by heart. Our elders taught us to seek help with those verses when faced with any kind of difficulty in any sort of situation. And whenever I did that, we got help; and if not, at least the anxiety subsided. This helped a great deal to lay the base of our beliefs in our religion. This was the phase that strengthened our faith to a great extent.

A Psalm of David

The Lord is my shepherd. I lack nothing. He makes me lie down in green pastures, he leads me beside quiet waters, He refreshes my soul. He guides me along the right paths for his name's sake. Even though I walk through the darkest valley, I will fear no evil, for you are with me; your rod and your staff, they comfort me.

You prepare a table before me in the presence of my enemies. You anoint my head with oil; my cup overflows. Surely your goodness and love will follow me all the days of my life, and I will dwell in the house of the Lord forever. (Psalm 23)

These were the verses that our grandmother Louise Dobyne made us learn by heart. These verses helped us a great deal in the trickiest of situations. These are the verse that provide immense support and strength to one's belief. These are the verses that still help me with whatever situation I am in. They help me no matter where I am and what age I am. They help me regardless of anything, and they comfort and soothe me with peace and harmony. Our elders always taught us to seek help from God and the verses He blessed us with rather than any other human being, who has no power over God's plan. This is what we always do, and this belief of ours has never let us down.

This, then, is how you should pray: "Our Father in heaven, hallowed be your name. Your kingdom come, you will be done on Earth as it is in heaven.

Give us today our daily bread. And forgive us our debts, as we also have forgiven our debtors. And lead us not into temptation, but deliver us from the evil one." (Matthew 6:9–13)

My First Spiritual Vision

Be strong and courageous. Do not be afraid or
*terrified because of them, for the L*ORD *your God goes*
with you; he will never leave you nor forsake you.
—Deuteronomy 31:6

THERE ARE THINGS happen in our life that make us terrified, and sometimes we don't know how to deal with them as they have never happened to us before. A similar sort of thing happened to me, and I had no clue how to even react as it was something that didn't happen with anyone in my proximity.

> Then you will know that I am in Israel,
> that I am the LORD your God, and that
> there is no other; never again will my
> people be shamed.

The Day of the LORD

And afterward, I will pour out my
Spirit on all people. Your sons and
daughters will prophesy, your old men
will dream dreams, your young men
will see visions. (Joel 2:27–28)

I had my first vision when I was about nineteen years old. I was a student of the DeVry Institute of Technology at that time. Along with attending college, I was working part-time at Twenty-Sixth Street in Chicago. It was in a Mexican community, and I was the first Black American to be employed in that particular community. The comfort I found was inexplicable. I found the people there to be so reassuring and uplifting that I loved every single moment I spent there. That was probably the only workplace that I waited to go to. My boss was the sweetest instructor I had ever met. She was more of a friend and mentor than a boss. She would spend time with me, reading the Bible. We used to discuss the verses and scriptures and talk about the things I had never discussed with anyone else. I was having a good time out there.

You alone are the LORD. You made the
heavens, even the highest heavens, and
all their starry host, the Earth and all

that is on it, the seas and all that is in them. You give life to everything, and the multitudes of heaven worship you. (Nehemiah 9:6)

Then a thing happened that I had never expected—not even in my wildest dreams! I had a vision! It happened one day when I was at home, lying in bed. I was just lost in a trail of my own thoughts. I had been thinking about what not and had been deeply indulged in it for quite some time. Just then, I had a thought. At first, I thought that it was just a very vivid thought. The vision I saw was of birds forming an image: the image of God's face in the air.

Through him, all things were made; without him, nothing was made that has been made. (John 1:3)

For in him all things were created: things in heaven and on earth, visible and invisible, whether thrones or powers or rulers or authorities; all things have been created through him and for him. (Colossians 1:16)

That was the day I realized maybe I was closer to God than I had ever anticipated. I had never thought this might come into my life. I was surprised, and more importantly, I was shocked. I had no idea I could be important or even visible to God. Yes, I had a firm belief in God and my religion, but to me, I had done nothing that could be rendered dear to God. To me, I was just an ordinary human and a believer like any other person. However, this thing made me think twice, as if maybe I was not *that* unimportant to God. Maybe I was something, and maybe I held my place, which even I was not aware of.

> God is spirit, and his worshipers must worship in the Spirit and in truth. (John 4:24)

Some things never change and stay attached to you. I used to watch the same dream over for days and sometimes for weeks. And just like that, the succession of peculiar dreams stayed with me. Some of them, I remember, while the others slipped from my mind. But there was this one very unusual dream. I still remember it and especially what followed it. That was, no doubt, the most unforgettable dream of my life.

> In peace I will lie down and sleep, for you alone, Lord, make me dwell in safety. (Psalm 4:8)

Around almost the entire time period between age eight and thirteen or fourteen, there was one dream that I used to see quite regularly. Almost every night for years, I was riding a tricycle; and when I reached the curve in the path, the tricycle turned over, causing me to fall off. This dream would put me on edge as the feeling of falling off from somewhere is itself a frightening sensation, and on top of that, I never saw the end of my descent. I never hit bottom, which made the dream more terrifying as there was never an end. I would be falling into deep depths and waking up in the middle of that. This one dream had the potential to keep me up for hours. I would lie in my bed with my eyes wide open in the middle of the night, my heart pounding in my chest, and I would wonder when it would stop. That one dream gave me a really hard time.

> "No weapon forged against you will prevail, and you will refute every tongue that accuses you. This is the heritage of the servants of the Lord, and this is their vindication from me," declares the Lord. (Isaiah 54:17)

The dream was probably an outcome of my depression and anxiety from the decisions I was making. But neither that dream nor the thought of it left me—not until I was in my first year. I had been driving a truck that was loaded with eighty thousand pounds and was over eighty feet in length. Everything was fine when all of a sudden, I steered the truck to take a quick curve and totaled the truck. The accident that happened was quite a major one, considering the mirror that was totally bent. But seeing me, none could recognize I had been a part of that disastrous event as there were no major injuries or damages I acquired. Along with all the people who witnessed the enormity of that event, I, too, was forced to think that it was as if the hand of God had been laid down on that vehicle and me. I was convinced, actually.

> Peace I leave with you; my peace I give you. I do not give to you as the world gives. Do not let your hearts be troubled, and do not be afraid. (John 14:27)

This incident helped prosper my belief that I was probably a dear one to God—that perhaps because of all the anguish I endured as a little child, now fruits were being borne for me in my adulthood.

> For though the righteous fall seven times, they rise again, but the wicked stumble when calamity strikes. (Proverbs 24:16)

I had passed my test, and now was the time where God would reward me with His blessings and mercy. Now I was not desolate, the way I used to be. I now had good thoughts, and more importantly, I had hope.

> For I am the Lord your God who
> takes hold of your right hand and says
> to you, Do not fear; I will help you.
> (Isaiah 41:13)

> No harm will overtake you, no disaster
> will come near your tent. (Psalm 91:10)

Lust

WE HUMANS ARE strange creatures. Whatever we say or declare, we do the exact opposite of. Our actions entirely contradict our words. We say something, and then we do something else. This is human nature in its original state. We are, perhaps, the most contradictory living being in this world.

Lord, as His nature is, provides and helps with the situation of that affected individual. Humans cry when met with a challenge that is not in their hands; they wail and call on the Lord. Man sees the approaching aid and gets euphoric at the relief of that wrath. Being obliged and grateful is what the following righteous action is, but man is churlish. Instead of correcting and admitting his wrongs, he reverts back to his former deeds, entirely forgetting how his Lord helped him out.

But still, the Lord provides even though the man was ever ungrateful.

> I am the vine; you are the branches. If you remain in me and I in you, you will bear much fruit; apart from me, you can do nothing. (John 15:5)

With the former experiences of the possession in my younger years, I was now terrified of anything close to this happening to me ever again. I had cried out to the Lord so many times to make the spirit go away from me at once. I had spent long nights crying my eyes out, remembering the dreadful experiences. I was imploring God day and night to banish that lustful spirit from me. It was really hard for me to be aware of its presence but still not be able to do anything about it. I wanted it to go away, and I needed it to go away. It was exasperating for me to deal with it the entire day. Lustful thoughts would consume me, and there was nothing I could do about it. I wanted to throw it out of me, but I did not know how. The spirit was far more potent than me, and all my efforts of expelling it were in vain.

Those were the days that I spent pleading to God. The spirit not only brought licentious thoughts but was also intoxicating enough to incline me toward alcohol and drugs. I was really apprehensive about my state.

The situation demanded that I get out of it without wasting any more time.

> Submit yourselves, then, to God. Resist the devil, and he will flee from you. (James 4:7)

The spirit continued to reside within me. The most appropriate action was to get attached to God so He would help me get rid of it. But I was a human too. Instead of completely submitting myself to God, I began modeling for local designer outfits with a fashion troop. Those guys were traveling from one state to another and even to other countries. I was twenty at that time, and life had morphed quite drastically from a religious one to this where fashion was the only means of living. This was the time where I was entirely living off and by fashion. It was my attire and my source of income as well.

Living in a world of fashion, I was still trying to control the lust under my own power. All those years ago, from my teens to then, I struggled with this thing. I had no power over the lustful desires that, once they began, would eventually come over and then consume me. I, having no power or authority over it, would succumb to them. Such thoughts were so commanding that I would soon lose control of myself.

Satan comes with deception. He knows what to do to make us lose. he knows every weakness of a fragile man and uses them to their fullest potential. The tactics are so carefully woven that a human is almost always certain to fall in them. The actuality of Satan's malicious schemes can be comprehended, remembering how he deluded Adam and Eve and got them place out of Garden of Eden. We are still just ordinary beings learning ways to cope in this deceiving world.

In 1985, I did a photoshoot. The outcome was to be placed at the water tower in downtown Chicago and the back cover of the *Chicago Defender* newspaper. I was aware it was not of God but still did it. I had lost my way, but I knew I would find my way back to Him one day or another.

> The thief comes only to steal and kill and destroy; I have come that they may have life and have it to the full. (John 10:10)

God Are You with Me/Fish Dinner

LIFE IS NOT always consistent. Some days, it goes up, while other days, it descends. A man cannot expect his entire life to be splendid and free from misery. If it were not for the dark days, how could we distinguish them from the good days? It is only darkness that makes us appreciate the light.

It was the year 2000. I was seeking God's cognizance. The fact that I was losing God and might get distant from Him made me distraught. Those days, I was struggling inside myself. There was a constant battle going on inside me.

I was driving from Georgia to Florida. There was a bridge, and while crossing it, I was talking to God the entire time. I was praying and pleading with God to show me some fishes jumping up out of the water under the bridge I was crossing. It was a peculiar wish, but I was constantly crying and praying while driving.

The last days had been really challenging for me, and I was constantly crying and imploring God to give me any sign that He was still with me. I felt that having any sort of indication from His side would perhaps cure the distress and anguish that I had been feeling for quite some time.

> God also said to Abraham, "As for Sarai your wife, you are no longer to call her Sarai; her name will be Sarah. I will bless her and will surely give you a son by her. I will bless her so that she will be the mother of nations; kings of peoples will come from her." (Genesis 17:15–16)

Abraham and Abimelek

> Now Abraham moved on from there into the region of the Negev and lived between Kadesh and Shur. For a while he stayed in Gerar, and there Abraham said of his wife Sarah, "She is my sister." Then Abimelek king of Gerar sent for Sarah and took her.
>
> But God came to Abimelek in a dream one night and said to him, "You are as good as dead because of the

woman you have taken; she is a married woman."

Now Abimelek had not gone near her, so he said, "Lord, will you destroy an innocent nation? Did he not say to me, 'She is my sister,' and didn't she also say, 'He is my brother'? I have done this with a clear conscience and clean hands."

Then God said to him in the dream, "Yes, I know you did this with a clear conscience, and so I have kept you from sinning against me. That is why I did not let you touch her. Now return the man's wife, for he is a prophet, and he will pray for you, and you will live. But if you do not return her, you may be sure that you and all who belong to you will die."

Early the next morning Abimelek summoned all his officials, and when he told them all that had happened, they were very much afraid.

Then Abimelek called Abraham in and said, "What have you done to us? How have I wronged you that you have brought such great guilt upon me and my kingdom? You have done things to me that should never be done."

And Abimelek asked Abraham, "What was your reason for doing this?"

Abraham replied, "I said to myself, 'There is surely no fear of God in this place, and they will kill me because of my wife. Besides, she really is my sister, the daughter of my father though not of my mother; and she became my wife.' And when God had me wander from my father's household, I said to her, 'This is how you can show your love to me: Everywhere we go, say of me, "He is my brother.""""

Then Abimelek brought sheep and cattle and male and female slaves and gave them to Abraham, and he returned Sarah his wife to him.

And Abimelek said, "My land is before you; live wherever you like."

To Sarah he said, "I am giving your brother a thousand shekels of silver. This is to cover the offense against you before all who are with you; you are completely vindicated." (Genesis 20:1–16)

I was in a relationship, and the fact was muddling for me, whether God approved of this relationship of mine or not. I was using the scriptures mentioned above as my foundation and ran out of clues on what to do next.

I was looking around for any sign from God that would ease my tension. I looked around for fish, but none were in sight. This lowered my spirits, and I began to pray more devotedly.

In Tennessee, I saw an accident scene. When I was returning from Florida, I was on Interstate 40, and something caught my eye. On asking, I got to know a truck driver had a heart attack while driving; and he drove off the interstate, landing in trees above the gorge. That person had been missing for three days and was nowhere to be found. The truck driver was then found in his truck, or perhaps the truck was seen hanging in the trees, as reported by some teenagers riding four-wheeler vehicles in the woods. This was how the accident was reported to the authorities, and the interstate was closed. The next day, troopers passed by that area; they took an alternative route and found out about the accident. The state troopers then posted sheets of paper on the interstate so that the travelers could take alternative routes. I was choosing the best route to reach my destination and took an alternative route. About a mile or less, I saw another accident happen at the curb. I pulled up to a state trooper directing the office and asked for his advice. It turned out he was a really rude person and answered me as if I would take his entire day. His discourtesy destroyed my mood, and I lost whatever control I was having over my disposition. I averted my car onto another route out of angst. I could not believe how someone could be this rude to a person who did nothing but probed a simple question politely.

The route I took out of angst led me into the Great Smoky Mountains of Tennessee. It was as if I had stepped into heaven, which had, itself, stepped on Earth. It was a tourist section of the mountain, and I can swear I had not seen anything close to the kind of beautiful it was. It was so striking that I had to remind myself that I was alive and standing in real life, observing reality. To my eyes, it was even grander than being exquisite and beautiful.

> The Lord himself goes before you and
> will be with you; he will never leave
> you nor forsake you. Do not be afraid;
> do not be discouraged. (Deuteronomy
> 31:8)

Seeing such a striking beauty, I felt the need to have a camera to capture the exquisite sights that were making me crazy. I instantly pulled over, parked, and ran inside a store connected to the ponds. I inquired if the store owner kept cameras and the tools used for the pond at his store. God answered my prayers. I prayed to see fishes jumping out of the water if He was still with me, and I did. The owner told me that they had a camera and the tools. He briefly explained they rented the fishing poles for catching fish; and if you liked, you could take the fish, the ones you caught, up to the restaurant. For they would cook it for you, and you could enjoy your fish meal there. It sounded like a brilliant idea, and this was exactly what I did. I was in dire need to do something like this and have some quality time for myself. So I did; I caught the fish by the mercy of God.

I asked God to provide me with good fish and show me how to catch them. God helped me with catching the fish, and I ate the food provided by God. After having what felt like the most pleasant meal of my life, I exclaimed, "Glory to God!"

> And if we know that he hears us—whatever we ask—we know that we have what we asked of him. (1 John 5:15)

Ask, Seek, Knock

> Ask, and it will be given to you; seek, and you will find; knock, and the door will be opened to you. For everyone

who asks receives; the one who seeks
finds; and to the one who knocks, the
door will be opened. (Matthew 7:7–8)

In the same year, I was off duty, so I planned one weekend to go out with my step-sister and a girlfriend of mine. We were going out for a drive to get high and have a good time. All three of us were high; we were laughing and cheering. We surely were having a great time—but not for long. After driving merrily for some time, I realized we had wandered into an area we were unfamiliar with. I had no clue where we were, nor did any of them know of our whereabouts. I was frustrated; what could I do in a situation like this to get us out? I was arguing with them even though they could do nothing, but I was getting exasperated because nothing was coming up. Neither of the two ladies were in a state to help me out. I did the only thing I knew could help me in such a state of affairs. I started to pray and ask God for a solution.

The moment I began my prayers was the same exact moment I was looking up at the sky. I was still angry and arguing with the girls, telling them they did not know the way and led me into this anonymous locality. Up there, a hawk caught my eye. I kept looking at the hawk and told them that I would take the hawk's help and follow it wherever it went since they did not know the way.

The fact that is the most interesting here is that the hawks usually do not stay visible for long and disappear from the view after some time. However, the hawk that I was staring at and followed further did stay within sight. I took it as God's mercy as it was unusual for me at that time and still is. The hawk stayed in my field of vision, and I kept following it for around ten minutes. After following the hawk for some time, I entered an area I was familiar with. It was no one but God who helped me that day and got me out of that situation. Glory to God.

> Trust in the Lord with all your heart
> and lean not on your own understand-
> ing; in all your ways, submit to him,
> and he will make your paths straight.
> (Proverbs 3:5–6)

We have this belief that since God gave us free will, it is up to us to choose what to do and where to go. It is true that God has given us the opportunity and ability to select things. This freedom is not granted to most of the creatures in this universe. Although He has given us this liberty to act as per our wishes, He wants us to choose His ways. This is what He wants—that we choose the ways that He likes for us. It is out of His love that He has left all things to our will and not imposed anything on us. In our assessment, we select the best possible option for ourselves and save ourselves from harm.

> But God demonstrates his own love for
> us in this: While we were still sinners,
> Christ died for us. (Romans 5:8)

God's Grace

THE ENTIRE TIME we were in Georgia, I witnessed God's grace and mercy being showered on me even more.

> The law was brought in so that the trespass might increase. But where sin increased, grace increased all the more. (Romans 5:20)

The love of my family followed me wherever I went. It never left me abandoned. Their constant moral, ethical, and financial support stayed with me irrespective of where I was. I was also blessed with their constant prayers, for which I deem myself quite fortunate. My mother never said no to me for anything, and this prevented any stranger or outsider from walking into my life in a negative way. No one could find a way to exploit me through my family, and God never left a void for anyone to fill.

This is the greatest blessing I have been rewarded with. I always mention and thank the Lord for always being blessed with people who uplift and support me. The few not-so-good people I've encountered are minute in number as compared to the good people I have in my life.

My dad died in 1995 from cancer. This was the most difficult time I have ever faced in my lifetime. I have always deeply loved my dad, and losing him was the biggest nightmare I ever encountered.

As a mother comforts her child, so will I comfort you; and you will be comforted over Jerusalem. (Isaiah 66:13)

Can a mother forget the baby at her breast and have no compassion on the child she has borne? Though she may forget, I will not forget you! (Isaiah 49:15)

Lilly is my first cousin. Evangelist Lagrant Dobyne was always there via phone. She always supported me through the prayers and encouragement that she blessed me with. She was the constant support system for me after my mom. Anytime I felt misery or distress, I went to share with her. Sharing everything with her and getting it off my chest provided me with great relief.

> Again, truly I tell you that if two of you on earth agree about anything they ask for, it will be done for them by my Father in heaven. For where two or three gather in my name, there am I with them. (Matthew 18:19–20)

> I urge, then, first of all, that petitions, prayers, intercession, and thanksgiving be made for all people. (1 Timothy 2:1)

> Therefore confess your sins to each other and pray for each other so that you may be healed. The prayer of a righteous person is powerful and effective. (James 5:16)

Right after 9/11, my step-sister and I decided to call off that relationship. It was sometime in the year 2001. I had asked her to take me to Creflo Dollar Ministries (World Changers Church International) for help. I had asked her this as she was the person I could trust. Never in the world could I have ever imagined what had happened next. If I had known what was going to come next for me, I would have run straight away from that, never once looking back.

While I was at Atlanta Victory Center, World Changers Ministry called and spoke with the pastor for Atlanta Victory Center. He had asked about how I was doing and requested me to come back and speak at World Changers to tell my testimony, to which the pastor said, "No." It was a really big thing for me to have been called by that ministry out of all the people. The pastor refused right away, saying, "You all would not take him in, and now you want him." I, on the other, had no clue of all this whatsoever until a week later when he mentioned this whole incident in a morning service. I just could not believe my ears that he would let pride and anger block the blessing of God. This was a great opportunity for me, but I could not participate in it as the pastor who could have handled it more responsibly had clogged the blessing. However, maybe a week later, I went back to my old ways, not trusting God and letting myself in without Jesus Christ. Even though I left, it did not take me long to return. But everything did not seem to be the same, so I left again. I just could not understand this; why was this happening to me after all?

Sometimes the most difficult task seems to be the one where you need to keep your head and heart on the same track. There are times where your head wanders off in the opposite direction from where your heart is.

It takes a while to get your bearings together as imposing anything on yourself, especially those related to religion, is just as useless as a sunflower seed for a mango plant. Therefore, I left myself for a while, patiently waiting for the will of God to guide me back to Him once again.

> "For I know the plans I have for you,"
> declares the Lord, "plans to prosper you
> and not to harm you, plans to give you
> hope and a future." (Jeremiah 29:11)

Life takes the most unexpected turns. It takes you to places you have never contemplated going before. Things were happening to me that I had no clue of. Life was going on fluidly, and it was as if I was oblivious of my existence or my well-being. The addictions never leave you in peace but surely leave you in bits and pieces. When you fall into the trap of addiction, dependence is easier and does not take much of a tussle. However, once you're inside the snare, it takes a lifetime to escape the spell of destruction.

I found myself homeless in Atlanta, with nowhere to go and nobody to go to. I was sleeping anywhere I could and eating anything I could find. Looking back, I wonder how I was able to keep going with my life. There was no light I could see in my life at that point when, out of nowhere, a ray of light entered my life.

It was God, and His grace showed up at just the right time. His grace motioned other homeless people who came to feed me almost regularly. On the other hand, God's grace directed me to places on the streets where ministries would outreach, such as Dr. Martin Luther King Jr.'s church, Ebenezer Baptist Church. These ministries would pass out lunch bags and meals to the homeless people living on the streets.

One day, someone told me about another halfway house for the addicted and homeless ones. It sounded like a good opportunity to me, so I went, and they took me in. It was a good initiative for people like me; but it turned out that it, too, was not going to work for me. By that time, I had completely fallen into the trap of addiction and continued to feed my addiction through any means possible.

I was still staying in the halfway house in Doraville, Georgia. It was one early morning when I came in from a binge and found everyone had gone to work. It was just me in the house, so I just decided to laze a little. The house had three floors, and I was staying in the lower part. The day had been tiring, so I was looking forward to just lying down in bed and easing my mind. As I was going to bed, my heart started beating fast, and I could not breathe. Things escalated really quickly, and soon I was unable to do anything. I wanted to call someone for help, but I could not. There was no phone I could call, so I tried to go upstairs. It seemed as if my heart was going to burst out, but I did not stop the struggle. Despite my efforts to bring back my strength, I still could not make it to the door. When nothing seemed to work, I decided to turn to God and ask Him to let me make it back downstairs to the bed. As I started walking back downstairs, I felt my pain subsiding. Thinking it was a positive sign, I turned around to go back up, but still, I was facing difficulty in it. So instead of doing it mightily, I decided to make it as slow as I now could at least move. Slowly making my way back down to the bed, I was saying, "God, if I die, I will die with You!"

With utmost struggle, I finally made it to bed, and a sigh of relief left my lungs. I covered my head and began pleading with the blood of Jesus over and over until the peace of God came over me, and soon enough, I went to sleep. That day, the love of God saved me from an overdose, or else I would not be sitting here, writing this book. All praise to God. I want to share some scriptures with my readers, to be used as strongholds.

> The Lord also will be a refuge for the oppressed, a refuge in times of trouble. And they that know thy name will put their trust in thee: for thou, Lord, hast not forsaken them that seek thee. (Psalm 9: 9–10)

For though we walk in the flesh, we do not war after the flesh: (For the weapons of our warfare are not carnal, but mighty through God to the pulling down of strong holds;) Casting down imaginations, and every high thing that exalteth itself against the knowledge of God, and bringing into captivity every thought to the obedience of Christ. (2 Corinthians 10:3–5)

For we wrestle not against flesh and blood, but against principalities, against powers, against the rulers of the darkness of this world, against spiritual wickedness in high places. (Ephesians 6:12)

The Lord hath made all things for himself: yea, even the wicked for the day of evil. (Proverbs 16:4)

Wherefore take unto you the whole armour of God, that ye may be able to withstand in the evil day, and having done all, to stand. Stand therefore, having your loins girt about with truth, and having on the breastplate of righteousness; and your feet shod with the preparation of the gospel of peace; above all, taking the shield of faith, wherewith ye shall be able to quench all the fiery darts of the wicked. And take the helmet of salvation, and the sword of the Spirit, which is the word of God: praying always with all prayer and supplication in the Spirit, and watching thereunto with all perseverance and supplication for all saints. (Ephesians 6:13–17)

One thing that stayed with me was my grandma and her words that remained deep-seated in my heart. She kept telling me never to go to Georgia or Florida, and she advised me never to go further away from home. Though I never really obeyed her words, her words kept lingering in the back of my mind and reminding me of the true place I belonged but had gone astray from. This all lasted for about a year and a half. I kept getting in and out of halfway homes in the state. From one home to another, from one door to another, I kept wandering, never once finding the right path.

Jesus answered and said unto him, Verily, verily, I say unto thee, Except a man be born again, he cannot see the kingdom of God.

Nicodemus saith unto him, How can a man be born when he is old? can he enter the second time into his mother's womb, and be born?

Jesus answered, Verily, verily, I say unto thee, Except a man be born of water and of the Spirit, he cannot enter into the kingdom of God.

That which is born of the flesh is flesh; and that which is born of the Spirit is spirit.

Marvel not that I said unto thee, Ye must be born again.

The wind bloweth where it listeth, and thou hearest the sound thereof, but canst not tell whence it cometh, and whither it goeth: so is everyone that is born of the Spirit.

Nicodemus answered and said unto him, How can these things be?

Jesus answered and said unto him, Art thou a master of Israel, and knowest not these things?

Verily, verily, I say unto thee, We speak that we do know, and testify that we have seen; and ye receive not our witness.

If I have told you earthly things, and ye believe not, how shall ye believe, if I tell you of heavenly things?

And no man hath ascended up to heaven, but he that came down from heaven, even the Son of man which is in heaven.

And as Moses lifted up the serpent in the wilderness, even so, must the Son of man be lifted up:

That whosoever believeth in him should not perish, but have eternal life.

For God so loved the world, that he gave his only begotten Son, that whosoever believeth in him should not perish, but have everlasting life.

For God sent not his Son into the world to condemn the world; but that the world through him might be saved.

He that believeth on him is not condemned: but he that believeth not is condemned already, because he hath not believed in the name of the only begotten Son of God.

And this is the condemnation, that light is come into the world, and men loved darkness rather than light, because their deeds were evil.

For every one that doeth evil hateth the light, neither cometh to the light, lest his deeds should be reproved.

But he that doeth truth cometh to the light, that his deeds may be made manifest, that they are wrought in God. (John 3:3–21)

God's Faithfulness

What advantage, then, is there in being a Jew, or what value is there in circumcision?

Much in every way! First of all, the Jews have been entrusted with the very words of God.

What if some were unfaithful? Will their unfaithfulness nullify God's faithfulness? Not at all! Let God be true, and every human being a liar. As it is written: "So that you may be proved right when you speak and prevail when you judge."

But if our unrighteousness brings out God's righteousness more clearly, what shall we say? That God is unjust in bringing his wrath on us? (I am using a human argument.)

Certainly not! If that were so, how could God judge the world?

Someone might argue, "If my falsehood enhances God's truthfulness, and so increases his glory, why am I still condemned as a sinner?"

Why not say—as some slanderously claim that we say—"Let us do evil that good may result"? Their condemnation is just!

No One Is Righteous

What shall we conclude then? Do we have any advantage? Not at all! For we have already made the charge that Jews and Gentiles alike are all under the power of sin.

As it is written:

"There is no one righteous, not even one; there is no one who understands; there is no one who seeks God. All have turned away, they have together become worthless; there is no one who does good, not even one."

"Their throats are open graves; their tongues practice deceit."

"The poison of vipers is on their lips."

"Their mouths are full of cursing and bitterness."

"Their feet are swift to shed blood; ruin and misery mark their ways, and the way of peace they do not know."

"There is no fear of God before their eyes."

Now we know that whatever the law says, it says to those who are under the law, so that every mouth may be silenced and the whole world held accountable to God.

Therefore no one will be declared righteous in God's sight by the works of the law; rather, through the law we become conscious of our sin.

Righteousness through Faith

But now, apart from the law, the righteousness of God has been made known, to which the Law and the Prophets testify.

This righteousness is given through faith in Jesus Christ to all who believe. There is no difference between Jew and Gentile, for all have sinned and fall short of the glory of God, and all are justified freely by his grace through the redemption that came by Christ Jesus.

God presented Christ as a sacrifice of atonement through the shedding of his blood—to be received by faith. He did this to demonstrate his righteousness because, in his forbearance, he had left the sins committed beforehand unpunished—he did it to demonstrate his righteousness at the present time so as to be just and the one who justifies those who have faith in Jesus.

Where, then, is boasting? It is excluded. Because of what law? The law that requires work? No, because of the law that requires faith.

For we maintain that a person is justified by faith apart from the works of the law.

Or is God the God of Jews only? Is he not the God of Gentiles too? Yes, of Gentiles too, since there is only one God, who will justify the circumcised by faith and the uncircumcised through that same faith.

Do we, then, nullify the law by this faith? Not at all! Rather, we uphold the law. (Romans 3:1–31)

For I am convinced that neither death nor life, neither angels nor demons, neither the present nor the future, nor any powers, neither height nor depth, nor anything else in all creation, will be able to separate us from the love of God that is in Christ Jesus our Lord. (Romans 8:38–39)

Trust God

WE OFTEN THINK aimlessly and keep fretting over the things that would eventually settle down one day or another. In our anxious and overthinking phase, we forget that there is an existence up there who had already planned out everything for us; He has laid out all things perfectly. His plan is not always comprehended by us, and it takes us a while to perceive that whatever loss it is that we are facing will surely lead us to something better.

This is about one night while I was staying in Doraville, Georgia. It was a halfway house that I was staying in. I was standing outside the house, smoking a cigarette, leaning against the building. I was constantly praying and asking God how He was going to get me out of this one. I was fretting and getting anxious over something that was a really trivial thing for God.

However, I am an ordinary human and was unaware of the plans Lord had laid out for me.

My prayers were answered in the most amazing way possible. I was not even finished with my prayers when I saw to my left a beautiful dark-skinned woman that came walking on the sidewalk. She was wearing a long white baseball sort of shirt and was coming out of her house. I saw her and walked up to her. I can say with chief honor that while going to her, I did not even have a speck of lustful feelings in my heart; it was pure and devoid of any impious thoughts. I initiated a conversation with her, and talking to her got me to know that she was heading to her car to get some groceries out, which she had left in the car earlier. I asked her if I could be of some use to her, and she said yes. Halfway back, she invited me to church. To my surprise, she told me to be ready in the morning, specifically at 5:00 a.m., with a shirt and tie on. It was a wonderful moment for me to be offered to visit the church by a beautiful woman to whom I could get attracted, but I did not. Instead, I was offered to go to church, which caught me by pleasant surprise. By the grace of God, I was perfectly ready by five in the morning, just as she had asked. One would think I was doing this for the sake of a woman when in reality, my heart was skipping beats on the fact that God had listened to my prayers and was calling me to provide answers.

When I was ready, I heard a knock at the door. A man informed me that Sister Blandy Deline—the woman God had sent for me—had instructed him to come and get me. I got out to see she had come to pick me up in her car. I rode with Sister Blandy while her husband was driving.

The entire time we were en route, my heart was bursting with happiness. The emotions I was hemmed in by that time are indescribable. I was feeling excited, happy, blissful, and blessed all at the same time. But most of all, a sense of contentment surrounded my entire existence; I was content that God was watching and listening to me. He had answered my prayers and not left me unaided.

I was cheerfully talking to Sister Blandy. It was so pleasant listening to her as I could relate to every word she said. It was later in the conversation when she revealed that she had a CD on which she sang. She told me that she had a gospel music CD, and for everything I was saying, she had a track. I found it really mesmerizing how she used music to articulate her thoughts and that they were helping a lot of people, especially people like me, who needed guidance and to whom just a little ray of sun was enough.

All of this was a form of validation from God. Yet another confirmation that I received from Him was when we were arriving at the church. Sister Blandy handed me a briefcase. She carried that book bag with her, in which she kept her Bible and other sermon materials for church service. She told me to take it and enter the church entrance through the left door. Her husband was watching every single move of mine and hers, but never did he utter a single word in any regard. He was just watching me through the rearview mirror. When we did arrive at the church, I glanced at the door on which the word *pastor* was inscribed. It was the moment I realized that I just had a ride with Sister Blandy and Pastor Deline in their car.

It is to this day that Pastor Deline of the Nation of Christ church, his wife Blandy Deline, and I became a family. Over the years, I found out how beautiful of a couple they are and how much of a gem of a person each of them individually are. They both are from Liberia, helping spread God's Word here. I deem myself truly blessed to have known them and be close to them.

> And it shall come to pass, that before they call, I will answer; and while they are yet speaking, I will hear. (Isaiah 65:24)

Pastor E. Deline is a genius person of his time. He was different from other pastors and could always be found indulged in something new that would carry a noble cause in itself. At the end of my stay there, Pastor E. Deline wrote a gospel play. The show was named "The Path." That show by Pastor E. Deline opened at the Fox Theater in Atlanta, Georgia, in the year 2005. That show held a significant value in recounting what he had in mind and wanted his friends to know.

I spent another six months in the Lazarus House. I was living there without giving any sort of money under the name of the rental fee, entirely free of cost. The only thing they ever asked of me was to keep studying the Word of God, which I was doing with utmost interest. I was always a very keen member and felt honored while fellowshipping with the other saints. Apart from religious studies, we were privileged enough to have access to other activities as well. We would play basketball, ping-pong, and similar plays to refresh our minds and keep our bodies active rather than become a bookworm devouring the Bible for the entire day. I always found it a good approach, and it definitely helped me shape my personality better.

As time passed, my grandmother Louise Dobyne passed away to be with a Lord. Not knowing how I was going to make it to the funeral, which wasn't in Alabama, I called my stepsister; and she took me, arriving in Alabama late to the funeral, moments before the lowering into the casket. I heard my mother saying, "Go ahead. He's not going to make it."

> Now faith is the substance of things hoped for, the evidence of things not seen. (Hebrews 11:1)

I returned to Chicago after attending the funeral. I began the quest for a job. I was aiming to get a truck driving job in Atlanta or neighboring cities of Atlanta. It was not much I was looking for, but sometimes even minimal things become challenging. I wanted to return to my Liberian family for church every Sunday if possible at Nation of Christ. My heart had found a profound connection with that church, and I wanted to keep that connection alive by visiting it every weekend.

Another thing I was yearning for and hoping to happen was to meet my wife. I was missing her, and now things felt quite mundane after having spent so many days without seeing her. It had been quite some time since I began searching for a job that would meet my requirements, but I was not yet successful in that quest of mine. Things seemed quite grim for some time, but giving some time for things to settle down makes them easier, facilitating in you gelling in with the circumstances.

The number six refers to many things in the Bible, but it's first mentioned in Genesis 1:31 when God created man on the sixth day.

> And God saw every thing that he had
> made, and, behold, it was very good.
> And the evening and the morning were
> the sixth day. (Genesis 1:31)

According to Bible scholars, just as the number seven typically signifies completion or perfection, especially of God, the number six is one shy of that, which means it signifies imperfection. More specifically, it refers to the imperfection of man and the sin and weakness he has.

> To the praise of the glory of his grace, wherein he hath made us accepted in the beloved. In whom we have redemption through his blood, the forgiveness of sins, according to the riches of his grace; wherein he hath abounded toward us in all wisdom and prudence; having made known unto us the mystery of his will, according to his good pleasure which he hath purposed in himself: That in the dispensation of the fulness of times he might gather together in one all things in Christ, both which are in heaven, and which are on earth; even in him: In whom also we have obtained an inheritance, being predestinated according to the purpose of him who worketh all things after the counsel of his own will: That we should be to the praise of his glory, who first trusted in Christ. (1 Peter 5:6–7)

Desires of your heart

> Take delight in the Lord, and he will give you the desires of your heart. Commit your way to the Lord; trust in him and he will do this. (Psalm 37:4–5)

> For where your treasure is, there will your heart be also. (Mathew 6:21)

> You have granted him his heart's desire and have not withheld the request of his lips. (Psalm 21:2)

> And we know that in all things, God works for the good of those who love him, who have been called according to his purpose. (Romans 8:28)

> For everyone who asks receives; the one who seeks finds; and to the one who knocks, the door will be opened. (Matthew 7:8)

It was a Sunday when I was at the Nation of Christ church. I was about to leave when I spotted a piece of paper under the wiper blade on the passenger side. I had not seen it until I got in the truck and was about to leave for the week. When I took it from under the wiper blade, I found it to be a phone number; it was from one of the church members. It was a lady, and her name was Jo Ann. Who could have thought that I would receive such a request from a beautiful woman? I was shocked to my core, and it was the most unexpected thing that could have happened to me. I have to admit I could not put my feet on earth that day.

Jo Ann was a lovely lady who worked in the kids' ministry. There, she was highly respected and known to be a pretty and professional lady. We had known each other since Lazarus House. I used to try to get her attention there, but she did not have it then. So I stopped my attempts to win her over and did not let that thing get to my head. And now here she was, back again in my life by making a move herself. It all seemed like the Lord's blessing on me, and I could not have been happier.

We dated for around six months while practicing abstinence. Apart from the kids' ministry, she was working two other jobs. I was proud of my lady; and every Friday, by the grace of God, I would go to her workplace with roses to show her she was my pride and the most beautiful thing to ever happen to me. I would see her bussing tables, and this made me love her even more. Seeing a woman working so hard for her family, being independent, and not relying on somebody else is something you don't get to see every day. I asked her to quit and said that I would help her with all that, but she refused and said she was doing it to buy a house for her kids, who were all grown up by then.

It took me a while, but I was finally able to talk her into quitting that job and taking a step ahead with me. We got engaged. Within a short while, all her endeavors came to fruition, and she bought the house. Every day, I would think this was the woman I had always been looking for. We were together for about two years, but we never got married. I don't know what came over me, but I ended up backsliding and started going back to my old ways. Whatever I was doing was unquestionably wrong, and I was going to lose what I had acquired by God's blessings on me.

This is for the men and women: Take care of your bodies because when that one person comes into your life whom God has sent for you and you really love, you will not be able to satisfy your mate because of the sexual sin unless you are ready to humble yourself to each other sexually irrespective to what sexual sin you have done to your body or has been done with your body. This love that God has chosen for you must be consummated with God in the center to keep it bound. It is not about finding the right person but recognizing them; and when they finally meet, regard them with honor, esteem, and respect.

Flee from sexual immorality. All other sins a person commits are outside the body, but whoever sins sexually, sins against their own body. Do you not know that your bodies are temples of the Holy Spirit, who is in you, whom you have received from God? You are not your own; you were bought at a price. Therefore honor God with your bodies. (1 Corinthians 6:18–20)

Marriage should be honored by all, and the marriage bed kept pure, for God will judge the adulterer and all the sexually immoral. (Hebrews 13:94)

But a man who commits adultery has no sense; whoever does so destroys himself. (Proverbs 6:32)

But since sexual immorality is occurring, each man should have sexual relations with his own wife, and each woman with her own husband. (1 Corinthians 7:2)

Jo Ann and I were together from 2004 till 2006. Unfortunately, she died in 2018. Her memories will forever stay ingrained deep in my mind, reminding me of our love for each other and the beautiful moments we spent together. I can never forget the love she had in her heart for life and people and all the goodness she had inside her. She had a lot more to offer to this world, and for the beautiful soul she was, this world lost a gem. God bless you, Jo Ann!

The Blood

CHRIST SHED HIS blood and died on the cross for our sins. Blood globally represents life itself.

> In whom we have redemption through his blood, the forgiveness of sins, according to the riches of his grace. (Ephesians 1:7)

> How much more shall the blood of Christ, who through the eternal Spirit offered himself without spot to God, purge your conscience from dead works to serve the living God? (Hebrews 9:14)

> For this is my blood of the new testament, which is shed for many for the remission of sins. (Matthew 26:28)

A Psalm of David

The Lord is my shepherd, I lack nothing. He makes me lie down in green pastures, he leads me beside quiet waters, he refreshes my soul. He guides me along the right paths for his name's sake. Even though I walk through the darkest valley, I will fear no evil, for you are with me; your rod and your staff, they comfort me. You prepare a table before me in the presence of my enemies. You anoint my head with oil; my cup overflows. Surely your goodness and love will follow me all the days of my life, and I will dwell in the house of the Lord forever. (Psalm 23:1–6)

In 2013, by the grace of God, I was awarded by Centerline an Anniversary Award (picture is attached).

Thomas Dobbins -- All in the Family!

As a young boy growing up on a farm in Alabama, Thomas drove trucks, tractors and all kinds of heavy machinery. Hard work was a way of life and one he enjoyed. He turned his love of truck driving into a 19-year career after receiving his CDL in 1993 at Chicago's Professional Truck Driving School.

Sometimes, however, life throws some curves. Physical injuries limited Thomas' ability to load and unload the cargo which in turn limited his driving opportunities.

With three sons and a daughter to support, he was motivated to reach out and try to find a partner that could understand while he had some limitations, he was a hard worker and motivated to succeed.

"Centerline had confidence in me and gave me a chance, Thomas recalled, "I had to prove myself, but with Centerline it's personal...they became like family. I didn't have to hide anything and because I didn't hide my physical limitations, I could be open to being blessed."

Thomas has been driving for Centerline since 2011 with one break for a full-time position, but he's back at Centerline to stay. His work with Vanessa and team has secured him long-term assignments that require that he only drive the trucks. "I couldn't believe how incredible my assignments have been! I can support my children, invest in my 401K and drive trucks, which is what I love to do!"

When asked what's the one thing you would tell a friend about Centerline he had a hard time narrowing to one great thing -- "I'd say they are great, never disrespectful, dependable and honest...they really and truly care about their drivers and customers! I could be a salesperson for Centerline - I love them that much!"

At Centerline we're glad Thomas is here to stay!

The following year, I had a hip replacement done in 2014 by the Rush hospital in Chicago. They did an awesome job, and by the grace of God, I was in fine fettle again.

And he spake a parable unto them to this end, that men ought always to pray, and not to faint;

Saying, There was in a city a judge, which feared not God, neither regarded man:

And there was a widow in that city; and she came unto him, saying, Avenge me of mine adversary.

And he would not for a while: but afterward he said within himself, Though I fear not God, nor regard man;

Yet because this widow troubleth me, I will avenge her, lest by her continual coming she weary me.

And the Lord said, Hear what the unjust judge saith.

And shall not God avenge his own elect, which cry day and night unto him, though he bear long with them?

I tell you that he will avenge them speedily. Nevertheless when the Son of man cometh, shall he find faith on the earth?

And he spoke this parable unto certain which trusted in themselves that they were righteous, and despised others:

Two men went up into the temple to pray; the one a Pharisee, and the other a publican.

The Pharisee stood and prayed thus with himself, God, I thank thee, that I am not as other men are, extortioners, unjust, adulterers, or even as this publican.

I fast twice in the week, I give tithes of all that I possess.

And the publican, standing afar off, would not lift up so much as his eyes unto heaven, but smote upon his breast, saying, God be merciful to me a sinner.

I tell you, this man went down to his house justified rather than the other: for everyone that exalteth himself shall be abased; and he that humbleth himself shall be exalted.

And they brought unto him also infants, that he would touch them: but when his disciples saw it, they rebuked them.

But Jesus called them unto him, and said, Suffer little children to come unto me, and forbid them not: for of such is the kingdom of God.

Verily I say unto you, Whosoever shall not receive the kingdom of God as a little child shall in no wise enter therein.

And a certain ruler asked him, saying, Good Master, what shall I do to inherit eternal life?

And Jesus said unto him, Why callest thou me good? None is good, save one, that is, God.

Thou knowest the commandments, Do not commit adultery, Do not kill, Do not steal, Do not bear false witness, Honour thy father and thy mother.

And he said, All these have I kept from my youth up.

Now when Jesus heard these things, he said unto him, Yet lackest thou one thing: sell all that thou hast, and distribute unto the poor, and thou shalt have treasure in heaven: and come, follow me.

And when he heard this, he was very sorrowful: for he was very rich.

And when Jesus saw that he was very sorrowful, he said, How hardly shall they that have riches enter into the kingdom of God!

For it is easier for a camel to go through a needle's eye, than for a rich man to enter into the kingdom of God.

And they that heard it said, Who then can be saved?

And he said, The things which are impossible with men are possible with God.

Then Peter said, Lo, we have left all, and followed thee.

And he said unto them, Verily I say unto you, There is no man that hath left house, or parents, or brethren, or wife, or children, for the kingdom of God's sake,

Who shall not receive manifold more in this present time, and in the world to come life everlasting. (Luke 18: 1–30)

It was the end of 2014 and around the beginning of 2015 when I was diagnosed with prostate cancer. While conducting various tests, what the doctors noticed was a hole the size of a quarter in one of my kidneys. I made up my mind to have my prostate removed, but during the pre-op, I informed the doctors that I had a migraine headache. This was not something normal, so the doctors were not able to do anything until a CT scan was performed.

My life was at a risky stage, and I didn't know what was going to happen next. I decided to be realistic and informed my insurance company, CountyCare. I went into the Rush hospital, only to hear them say that it was not approved by my insurance company. It was odd, so I called them, and they said it was approved. This felt like a relief, so I set up another appointment with the Rush hospital. I had gone there with the hopes that everything would be okay, but when I got there, they instead told me yet again that it was not approved.

I have never felt more discouraged in my life than I did then. Frustrated, I left the hospital, not returning or calling them again. Instead, I headed to the church that Sunday and prayed as I had never done before. I knew there was nothing and no one who could help me out in this situation but God. So I did what any disciple would do: pray to Him.

> And he said, A certain man had two sons:
> And the younger of them said to his father, Father, give me the portion of goods that falleth to me. And he divided unto them his living.
> And not many days after, the younger son gathered all together, and took his journey into a far country, and there wasted his substance with riotous living.

And when he had spent all, there arose a mighty famine in that land; and he began to be in want.

And he went and joined himself to a citizen of that country; and he sent him into his fields to feed swine.

And he would fain have filled his belly with the husks that the swine did eat: and no man gave unto him.

And when he came to himself, he said, How many hired servants of my father's have bread enough and to spare, and I perish with hunger!

I will arise and go to my father, and will say unto him, Father, I have sinned against heaven, and before thee,

And am no more worthy to be called thy son: make me as one of thy hired servants.

And he arose, and came to his father. But when he was yet a great way off, his father saw him, and had compassion, and ran, and fell on his neck, and kissed him.

And the son said unto him, Father, I have sinned against heaven, and in thy sight, and am no more worthy to be called thy son.

But the father said to his servants, Bring forth the best robe, and put it on him; and put a ring on his hand, and shoes on his feet:

And bring hither the fatted calf, and kill it; and let us eat, and be merry:

For this my son was dead, and is alive again; he was lost, and is found. And they began to be merry.

Now his elder son was in the field: and as he came and drew nigh to the house, he heard musick and dancing.

And he called one of the servants, and asked what these things meant.

And he said unto him, Thy brother is come; and thy father hath killed the fatted calf, because he hath received him safe and sound.

And he was angry, and would not go in: therefore came his father out, and intreated him.

And he answering said to his father, Lo, these many years do I serve thee, neither transgressed I at any time thy commandment: and yet thou never gavest me a kid, that I might make merry with my friends:

But as soon as this thy son was come, which hath devoured thy living with harlots, thou hast killed for him the fatted calf.

And he said unto him, Son, thou art ever with me, and all that I have is thine.

It was meet that we should make merry, and be glad: for this, thy brother was dead, and is alive again; and was lost, and is found. (Luke 15:11–32)

And if we know that he hear us, whatsoever we ask, we know that we have the petitions that we desired of him. (1 John 5:15)

For I know the thoughts that I think toward you, saith the Lord, thoughts of peace, and not of evil, to give you an expected end.

Then shall ye call upon me, and ye shall go and pray unto me, and I will hearken unto you.

And ye shall seek me, and find me, when ye shall search for me with all your heart. (Jeremiah 29:11–13)

I cried unto him with my mouth, and he was extolled with my tongue. If I regard iniquity in my heart, the Lord will not hear me: But verily God hath heard me; he hath attended to the voice of my prayer. Blessed be God, which hath not turned away my prayer, nor his mercy from me. (Psalm 66:17–20)

From 2006 to 2015, life was full of trials and tribulations as well as praying and quoting Psalm 23, Matthew 6:9–13, and Joshua 1:9. On July 1, 2015, I was staying with my mom and family, sitting in my room, listening to music, drinking, and smoking a cigarette. All at once, time stopped, and then I saw an image of God's face and three scriptures in front of my face. Both the visions were blurry, and He whispered in my right ear, "Honor your mother love your mother, and obey your mother." As soon as the last word was spoken, time started, and I didn't recall having the vision.

I got up and left the house that evening. I returned on Saturday morning, on the Fourth of July, at around 5:00 a.m., by the grace of God. I then sat in a chair across from my mother, who was in the dining room, where she had been sleeping on a love seat since 1995, after my dad died (crossover).

I said, "Mama! Mama."

She answered, "What?"

I said, "I love you."

She said, "I don't know why you keep saying that and doing the things you do."

As she was speaking and moving toward the kitchen, God returned the vision to my mind, and I said, "Mama, I had a vision about everything you just said." As God revealed more of the vision, I started crying and talking.

At about 10:00 a.m., Paul Ward, my dad and mom's best friend since I was a child, came over, and he'd never come to our house that early before. As he heard me speak, he commented; and when he did, God revealed even more of the vision. The power the Holy Spirit had over me was so strong that all I could do was glorify God, saying, "What if the power of God changed the particular woman in the neighborhood? How many souls she could save!" The Holy Spirit had me thinking about others before myself. Around 12:00 p.m., I was exhausted and went to sleep, promising to return to church. The next day, God had removed the desire for alcohol, drugs, and cigarettes. The other time He did that was when I was in Georgia, at Atlanta Victory Center and the Nation of Christ. Looking back, each time, it only lasted for six months.

> Jesus looked at them and said, "With
> man, this is impossible, but with God,
> all things are possible." (Matthew 19:26)

I can do all things through him who strengthens me. (Philippians 4:13)

If we are faithless, He remains faithful, for he cannot disown himself. (2 Timothy 2:13)

And afterwards, I will pour out my Spirit on all people. Your sons and daughters will prophesy, your old men will dream dreams, and your young men will see visions. Even on my servants, both men and women, I will pour out my Spirit in those days. (Joel 2:28–29)

In the month of December 2015, I met a woman on a social media website instead of trusting God's Word and being obedient to God's will! I was lonely and desired to love, so I dedicated all my time to her! My family and my mom especially said, "Can't you see she's pulling you away from God?" I had chosen her or my lust over God, and even though she stayed in another country, I was in love.

Mr. Paul Ward came over one day and asked me not to talk to her for three weeks. I got upset and said I couldn't do that to her or myself. Considering who he was to my family, I gave him the benefit of the doubt and gave him three hours. She was constantly calling, but I wouldn't answer. It was hard, and I didn't understand what was going on. He never did explain why! When we finally talked, things weren't the same, and I mean they were totally different! My heart was broken, and I never did want to see the truth.

The relationship lasted about two or three more years. And by that time, I had started smoking again. I was so broken I went to God to pray and said, "Lord, forgive me, but I'm laying down what You've done for me, and by Your grace, I'll need You to put it back on me when I ask in Jesus Christ's holy name." This shows how broken I was! It didn't take long for the drugs and alcohol to resurface again. Then I received a revelation that His vision was a warning. Prior to meeting her, I'd never worn a Bluetooth, but I wore it in the same ear the spirit of God whispered, "Honor your mother, love your mother, and obey your mother." I still couldn't pull myself away! God, being who He is, blessed me to go and visit her twice, and He also blessed me not to use drugs or alcohol either time. I was in love and broken in Spirit…

> Do not be unequally yoked together with unbelievers. For what fellowship has righteousness with lawlessness? And what communion has light with darkness? (2 Corinthians 6:14)

Do not love the world or the things in the world. If anyone loves the world, the love of the Father is not in him. For all that is in the world—the lust of the flesh, the lust of the eyes, and the pride of life—is not of the Father but is of the world. And the world is passing away, and the lust of it; but he who does the will of God abides forever. (1 John 2:15–17)

Blessed is the man who endures temptation, for when he has been approved, he will receive the crown of life which the Lord has promised to those who love Him. Let no one say when he is tempted, "I am tempted by God"; for God cannot be tempted by evil, nor does He Himself tempt anyone. But each one is tempted when he is drawn away by his own desires and enticed. Then, when desire has conceived, it gives birth to sin; and sin, when it is full-grown, brings forth death. (James 1:12–17)

Do not be deceived, my beloved brethren. Every good gift and every perfect gift is from above and comes down from the Father of lights, with whom there is no variation or shadow of turning. (James 1:16–18)

Let us walk properly, as in the day, not in revelry and drunkenness, not in lewdness and lust, not in strife and envy. But put on the Lord Jesus Christ, and make no provision for the flesh, to fulfill its lusts. (Romans 13:13–14)

For the flesh lusts against the Spirit, and the Spirit against the flesh; and these are contrary to one another so that you do not do the things that you wish. (Galatians 5:17)

The Lord is near to those who have a broken heart. And saves such as have a contrite spirit. (Psalm 34:18)

But God demonstrates His own love toward us, in that while we were still sinners, Christ died for us. (Romans 5:8)

Thank you, our father, and my Lord and Savior Jesus Christ: "Now the

Spirit expressly says that in latter times some will depart from the faith, giving heed to deceiving spirits and doctrines of demons." (1 Timothy 4:1)

Be sober, be vigilant; because your adversary the devil walks about like a roaring lion, seeking whom he may devour. (1 Peter 5:8)

Love for God and one another

Beloved, do not believe every Spirit, but test the spirits, whether they are of God; because many false prophets have gone out into the world. By this, you know the Spirit of God: Every Spirit that confesses that Jesus Christ has come in the flesh is of God, and every Spirit that does not confess that Jesus Christ has come in the flesh is not of God. And this is the Spirit of the Antichrist, which you have heard was coming and is now already in the world. You are of God, little children, and have overcome them because He who is in you is greater than he who is in the world. They are of the world. Therefore they

speak as of the world, and the world
hears them. (1 John 4:1–5)

One Sunday morning, I was lying on our couch, and a vision came. It was of a demon in front of me, swaying from side to side. His face would change. He'd also back up as he swayed until he faded into the darkness, and I wondered why he left. I looked behind me, and I saw Jesus dressed in divine glory. Then I said, "That's why he left!"

When God shows you something, your first reaction is to tell someone. I couldn't just call anybody, but since God put Paul Ward in my spirit, I called him. He answered and asked what time it was.

"It's 5:00 a.m."

He said, "I'm glad you called! I'm late for church!"

This was my confirmation this was of God.

For God is not the author of confusion
but of peace, as in all the churches of
the saints. (1 Corinthians 14:33)

Four years later, God revealed these three scriptures, which were blurry in the 2015 vision to me. They are as follows:

- James 4:10
- 1 Peter 5:6–7

Humble yourselves in the sight of the Lord, and He will lift you up. (James 4:10)

Therefore humble yourselves under the mighty hand of God, that He may exalt you in due time, casting all your care upon Him, for He cares for you. (1 Peter 5:6–7)

Casting down imaginations and every high thing that exalteth itself against the knowledge of God, and bringing into captivity every thought to the obedience of Christ. (2 Corinthians 10:5)

For the wages of sin is death, but the gift of God is eternal life through Jesus Christ our Lord. (Romans 6:23)

If we confess our sins, He is faithful and just to forgive us our sins and to cleanse us from all unrighteousness. (1 John 1:9)

And why call ye Me, 'Lord, Lord,' and do not the things which I say? (Luke 6:46)

Then Peter and the other apostles answered and said, "We ought to obey God rather than men. (Acts 5:29)

But if ye will not obey the voice of the Lord, but rebel against the commandment of the Lord, then shall the hand of the Lord be against you, as it was against your fathers. (1 Samuel 12:15)

For men shall be lovers of their own selves, covetous, boasters, proud, blasphemers, disobedient to parents. (2 Timothy 3:2)

Children, obey your parents in all things, for this is well-pleasing unto the Lord. (Colossians 3:20)

One late (or was it early?) morning, I left a neighborhood outside of Chicago where I was doing drugs and headed to a hotel with a woman. Two cars pulled up behind me and started shooting. The first bullet hit my back windshield, shattering it.

The woman with me started hollering, "They're shooting at you!"

From that point on, I didn't hear another sound. God dropped in my spirit the vision of the demon that was swaying side to side seven years earlier, so I slowed down and started swaying my car side to side. I still did not hear any sounds, not even a gun firing, then one of the bullets grazed my left earlobe, leaving it hot as both cars passed, still shooting. I slowed down even more with all my windows shot out except the front windshield. As the last car passed, I started to T-bone it, but the spirit of God said, "Let me have the glory." So I backed off, and the woman jumped out and ran.

What is salvation?

Salvation is about being delivered from that which can injure or destroy. When someone is in danger and gets rescued or is suffering and gets relief, it is said that he has been saved. But Christian salvation is about far more. It is victory in Jesus, spiritual wellness, and the gift of eternal life.

First and foremost, God wants each person to come to a saving knowledge of Jesus Christ through faith in His work on the cross and resurrection. Peter wrote to a group of churches, "The Lord is not slow to fulfill his promise as some count slowness, but is patient toward you, not wishing that any should perish, but that all should reach repentance" (2 Peter 3:9). This is why God does not hasten the end of this time period before the tribulation and final judgment. He wants to give as much time as possible for as many souls as possible to accept the free gift of salvation through Jesus.

> And they overcame him by the blood of
> the Lamb and by the word of their tes-
> timony, and they loved not their lives
> unto the death. (Revelation 12:11)

> For by grace are ye saved through faith,
> and that not of yourselves: it is the gift
> of God—not by works, lest any man
> should boast. (Ephesians 2:8–9)

Glory to God!

My mother, Clara L. Dobbins, crossed over. She loved me with the love of God from birth and treated me as God has—with love, grace, and mercy. She met her Lord and Savior, Jesus Christ. I love you, Mama!

> He that findeth his life shall lose it; and
> he that loseth his life for My sake, shall
> find it. (Matthew 10:39)

Thank you, Father, for complete deliverance from drugs and sins of the flesh. In Jesus Christ's holy name, I pray.

> If My people, who are called by My name, shall humble themselves and pray, and seek My face and turn from their wicked ways, then will I hear from heaven, and will forgive their sin and will heal their land. (2 Chronicles 7:14)

> For His anger endureth but a moment, and in His favor is life; weeping may endure for a night, but joy cometh in the morning. (Psalm 30:5)

> For we are His workmanship, created in Christ Jesus unto good works, which God hath beforehand ordained, that we should walk in them. (Ephesians 2:10)

> And be ye kind one to another, tenderhearted, forgiving one another, even as God for Christ's sake hath forgiven you. (Ephesians 4:32)

Recompense no man evil for evil. Provide things honest in the sight of all men. (Romans 12:17)

A new commandment I give unto you: that ye love one another, as I have loved you, that ye also love one another. (John 13:34)

Then Peter came to Him and said, "Lord, how often shall my brother sin against me, and I forgive him? Until seven times?" And Jesus said unto him, "I say not unto thee, until seven times, but until seventy times seven." (Matthew 18:21–22)

This is My commandment: that ye love one another, as I have loved you. (John 15:12)

And we have known and believed the love that God hath for us. God is love, and he that dwelleth in love dwelleth in God, and God in him. (1 John 4:16)

"Comfort ye, comfort ye My people," saith your God. (Isaiah 40:1)

"Speak ye comfortingly to Jerusalem, and cry unto her that her warfare is accomplished, that her iniquity is pardoned; for she hath received from the Lord's hand double for all her sins."

The voice of him that crieth in the wilderness: "Prepare ye the way of the Lord; make straight in the desert a highway for our God. Every valley shall be exalted, and every mountain and hill shall be made low, and the crooked shall be made straight, and the rough places plain. And the glory of the Lord shall be revealed, and all flesh shall see it together; for the mouth of the Lord hath spoken it."

The voice said, "Cry!" And he said, "What shall I cry?"

"All flesh is grass, and all the goodliness thereof is as the flower of the field. The grass withereth, the flower fadeth, because the spirit of the Lord bloweth upon it; surely the people is grass. The grass withereth, the flower fadeth; but the word of our God shall stand forever."

O Zion that bringest good tidings get thee up into the high mountain; O

Jerusalem, that bringest good tidings, lift up thy voice with strength. Lift it up, be not afraid; say unto the cities of Judah, "Behold your God!"

Behold, the Lord God will come with a strong hand, and His arm shall rule for Him; behold, His reward is with Him, and His work before Him. He shall feed His flock like a shepherd; He shall gather the lambs with His arm and carry them in His bosom, and shall gently lead those that are with young.

Who hath measured the waters in the hollow of His hand, and meted out heaven with the span, and comprehended the dust of the earth in a measure, and weighed the mountains in scales and the hills in a balance? Who hath directed the Spirit of the Lord, or being His counselor hath taught Him? With whom took He counsel, and who instructed Him, and taught Him in the path of judgment, and taught Him knowledge, and showed to Him the way of understanding?

Behold, the nations are as a drop of a bucket and are counted as the small dust of the balance; behold, He taketh up the isles as a very little thing. And Lebanon is not sufficient to burn, nor the beasts thereof sufficient for a burnt offering. All nations before Him are as nothing, and they are counted to Him less than nothing, and vanity.

To whom then will ye liken God? Or what likeness will ye compare unto Him? The workman melteth a graven image, and the goldsmith spreadeth it over with gold and casteth silver chains. He that is so impoverished that he hath no oblation chooseth a tree that will not rot; he seeketh unto him a skillful workman to prepare a graven image that shall not be moved.

Have ye not known? Have ye not heard? Hath it not been told you from the beginning? Have ye not understood from the foundations of the earth?

It is He that sitteth upon the circle of the earth, and the inhabitants thereof are as grasshoppers, who stretcheth out the heavens as a curtain and spreadeth them out as a tent to dwell in,

Who bringeth the princes to nothing; He maketh the judges of the earth as vanity.

Yea, they shall not be planted, yea, they shall not be sown; yea, their stock shall not take root in the earth. And He shall also blow upon them, and they shall wither, and the whirlwind shall take them away as stubble.

To whom then will ye liken Me, or shall I be equal?" saith the Holy One.

Lift up your eyes on high and behold who hath created these things, who bringeth out their host by number. He calleth them all by names by the greatness of His might, for He is strong in power; not one faileth.

Why sayest thou, O Jacob, and speakest, O Israel: "My way is hid from the Lord, and my judgment is passed over from my God"?

Hast thou not known? Hast thou not heard that the everlasting God, the Lord, the Creator of the ends of the earth, fainteth not, neither is weary? There is no searching for His understanding.

He giveth power to the faint, and to them that have no might He increaseth strength.

Even the youths shall faint and be weary, and the young men shall utterly fall; but they that wait upon the Lord shall renew their strength; they shall mount up with wings as eagles, they shall run and not be weary, and they shall walk and not faint. (Isaiah 40:2–31)

For by grace are ye saved through faith, and that not of yourselves: it is the gift of God— not by works, lest any man should boast. (Ephesians 2:8–9)

I am the vine, ye are the branches. He that abideth in Me and I in Him, the same bringeth forth much fruit, for without Me ye can do nothing. (John 15:5)

Have not I commanded thee? Be strong and of good courage; be not afraid, neither be thou dismayed, for the Lord thy God is with thee whithersoever thou goest. (Joshua 1:9)

My mother and father honored and loved their family! And they loved God.

If a man says, "I love God," and hateth his brother, he is a liar. For he that loveth not his brother whom he hath seen, how can he love God whom he hath not seen? (1 John 4:20)

Honor and glory to God the Highest and my Lord and Savior, Jesus Christ.

Therefore, since we have been justified through faith, we have peace with God through our Lord Jesus Christ. Through him, we have gained access by faith into this grace in which we now stand. And we boast in the hope of the glory of God. Not only so, but we also glory in our sufferings because we know that suffering produces perseverance; perseverance produces character, and character produces hope, and hope does not put us to shame because God's love has been poured out into our hearts through the Holy Spirit, who has been given to us. (Romans 5:1–11 ESV)

And we know that all things work together for good to them that love God, to them who are the called according to his purpose. (Romans 8:28 KJV)

Resting in Christ Jesus

Flee from sexual immorality. All other sins a person commits are outside the body, but whoever sins sexually, sins against their own body. Do you not know that your bodies are temples of the Holy Spirit, who is in you, whom you have received from God? You are not your own; you were bought at a price. Therefore honor God with your bodies. (1 Corinthians 6:18–20 NIV)

Doing Good to All

Brothers and sisters, if someone is caught in a sin, you who live by the Spirit should restore that person gently. But watch yourselves, or you also may be tempted. Carry each other's burdens, and in this way you will fulfill the law of Christ. If anyone thinks they are something when they are not, they deceive themselves. Each one should test their own actions. Then they can take pride in themselves alone, without comparing themselves to someone else, for each one should carry their own load. Nevertheless, the one who receives instruction in the word should share all good things with their instructor.

Do not be deceived: God cannot be mocked. A man reaps what he sows. Whoever sows to please their flesh, from the flesh will reap destruction; whoever sows to please the Spirit, from the Spirit will reap eternal life. Let us not become weary in doing good, for at the proper time we will reap a harvest if we do not give up. (Galatians 6:1–9 NIV)

Watch and pray so that you will not fall into temptation. The spirit is willing, but the flesh is weak. (Matthew 26:41 NIV)

Life by the Spirit

You, my brothers and sisters, were called to be free. But do not use your freedom to indulge the flesh; rather, serve one another humbly in love. For the entire law is fulfilled in keeping this one command: "Love your neighbor as yourself." If you bite and devour each other, watch out or you will be destroyed by each other.

So I say, walk by the Spirit, and you will not gratify the desires of the flesh. For the flesh desires what is contrary to the Spirit, and the Spirit what is contrary to the flesh. They are in conflict with each other, so that you are not to do whatever you want. But if you are led by the Spirit, you are not under the law.

The acts of the flesh are obvious: sexual immorality, impurity and debauchery; idolatry and witchcraft; hatred, discord, jealousy, fits of rage, selfish ambition, dissensions, factions and envy; drunkenness, orgies, and the like. I warn you, as I did before, that those who live like this will not inherit the kingdom of God. (Galatians 5:13–21 NIV)

Put on the full armor of God, so that you can take your stand against the devil's schemes. For our struggle is not against flesh and blood, but against the rulers, against the authorities, against the powers of this dark world and against the spiritual forces of evil in the heavenly realms. Therefore put on the full armor of God, so that when the day of evil comes, you may be able to stand your ground, and after you have done everything, to stand. Stand firm then, with the belt of truth buckled around your waist, with the breastplate of righteousness in place, and with your feet fitted with the readiness that comes from the gospel of peace. In addition to all this, take up the shield of faith, with which you can extinguish all the flaming arrows of the evil one. Take the helmet of salvation and the sword of the Spirit, which is the word of God.

And pray in the Dobbins on all occasions with all kinds of prayers and requests. With this in mind, be alert and always keep on praying for all the Lord's people. (Ephesians 6:11–18 NIV)

Remain in me, as I also remain in you. No branch can bear fruit by itself; it must remain in the vine. Neither can you bear fruit unless you remain in me.

I am the vine; you are the branches. If you remain in me and I in you, you will bear much fruit; apart from me you can do nothing. If you do not remain in me, you are like a branch that is thrown away and withers; such branches are picked up, thrown into the fire and burned. If you remain in me and my words remain in you, ask whatever you wish, and it will be done for you. This is to my Father's glory, that you bear much fruit, showing yourselves to be my disciples.

As the Father has loved me, so have I loved you. Now remain in my love. If you keep my commands, you will remain in my love, just as I have kept my Father's commands and remain in his love. I have told you this so that my joy may be in you and that your joy may be complete. My command is this: Love each other as I have loved you. Greater love has no one than this: to lay down one's life for one's friends. You are my friends if you do what I command. I no longer call you servants, because a servant does not know his master's business. Instead, I have called you friends, for everything that I learned from my Father I have made known to you. You did not choose me, but I chose you and appointed you so that you might go and bear fruit—fruit that will last—and so that whatever you ask in my name the Father will give you. This is my command: Love each other. (John 15:4–17 NIV)

Give thanks to the Lord, for he is good; his love endures forever. Let the redeemed of the Lord tell their story— those he redeemed from the hand of the foe, those he gathered from the lands, from east and west, from north and south. Some wandered in desert wastelands, finding no way to a city where they could settle. They were hungry and thirsty, and their lives ebbed away.

Then they cried out to the Lord in their trouble, and he delivered them from their distress. He led them by a straight way to a city where they could settle. Let them give thanks to the Lord for his unfailing love and his wonderful deeds for mankind, for he satisfies the thirsty and fills the hungry with good things. Some sat in darkness, in utter darkness, prisoners suffering in iron chains, because they rebelled against God's commands and despised the plans of the Most High. So he subjected them to bitter labor; they stumbled, and there was no one to help. Then they cried to the Lord in their trouble, and he saved them from their distress. He brought them out of darkness, the utter darkness, and broke away their chains. Let them give thanks to the Lord for his unfailing love and his wonderful deeds for mankind, for he breaks down gates of bronze and cuts through bars of iron. Some became fools through their rebellious ways and suffered affliction because of their iniquities. They loathed all food and drew near the gates of death. Then they cried to the Lord in their trouble, and he saved them from their distress. He sent out his word and healed them; he rescued them from the grave. Let them give thanks to the Lord for his unfailing love and his wonderful deeds for mankind. Let them sacrifice thank offerings and tell of his works with songs of joy. Some went out on the sea in ships; they were merchants on the mighty waters. They saw the works of the Lord, his wonderful deeds in the deep. For he spoke and stirred up a tempest that lifted high the waves. They mounted up to the heavens and went down to the depths; in their peril their courage melted away. They reeled and staggered like drunkards; they were at their wits' end. Then they cried out to the Lord in their trouble, and he brought them out of their distress. He stilled the storm to a whisper; the waves of the sea were hushed. They were glad when it grew calm, and he guided them to their desired haven. Let them give thanks to the Lord for his unfailing love and his wonderful deeds for mankind. Let them exalt him in the assembly of the people and praise him in the council of the elders. He turned rivers into a desert, flowing springs into thirsty ground, and fruitful land into a salt waste, because of the wickedness of those who lived there. He turned the desert into pools of water and the parched ground into flowing springs; there he brought the hungry to live, and they founded a city where they could settle. They sowed fields and planted vineyards that yielded a fruitful harvest; he blessed them, and their numbers greatly increased, and he did not let their herds diminish. Then their numbers decreased, and they were humbled by oppression, calamity and sorrow; he who pours contempt on nobles made them wander in a trackless waste. But he lifted the needy out of their affliction and increased their families like flocks. The upright see and rejoice, but all the wicked shut their mouths. Let the one who is wise heed these things and ponder the loving deeds of the Lord. (Psalm 107)

Afterword

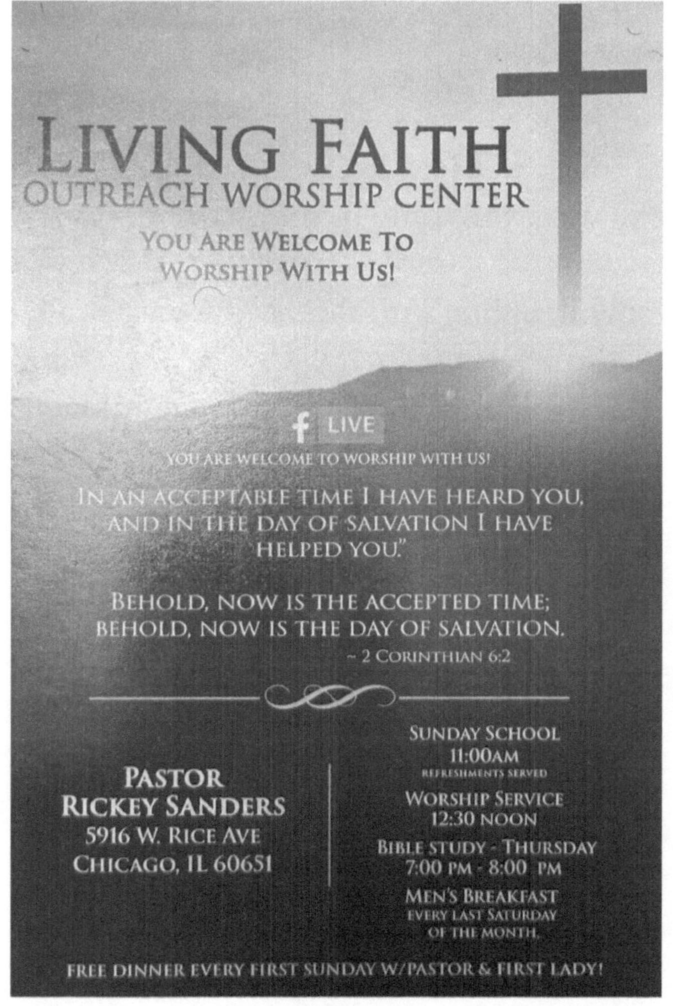

LIVING FAITH
OUTREACH WORSHIP CENTER
YOU ARE WELCOME TO
WORSHIP WITH US!

LIVE
YOU ARE WELCOME TO WORSHIP WITH US!

IN AN ACCEPTABLE TIME I HAVE HEARD YOU,
AND IN THE DAY OF SALVATION I HAVE
HELPED YOU."

BEHOLD, NOW IS THE ACCEPTED TIME;
BEHOLD, NOW IS THE DAY OF SALVATION.
~ 2 CORINTHIAN 6:2

PASTOR
RICKEY SANDERS
5916 W. RICE AVE
CHICAGO, IL 60651

SUNDAY SCHOOL
11:00AM
REFRESHMENTS SERVED

WORSHIP SERVICE
12:30 NOON

BIBLE STUDY - THURSDAY
7:00 PM - 8:00 PM

MEN'S BREAKFAST
EVERY LAST SATURDAY
OF THE MONTH.

FREE DINNER EVERY FIRST SUNDAY W/PASTOR & FIRST LADY!

BLESSINGS GO OUT to the angels God placed in my life that nurtured me in songs and prayers:

- my daughter's mother, Irene Vance
- Pastor/Evangelist Lillie Dobyne Lagrant
- Pastor (Evangelist) Virginia Desmuke
- Evangelist Blandy, her husband Pastor E. Deline with the Nation of Christ, Gwen Callaway (thank you for your prayer box), and Pastor Rickey Sanders.
- most of all, my mom, Clara L Dobbins

Love you all with the love of God!

Are they not all ministering spirits, sent forth to minister for them who shall be heirs of salvation? (Hebrew 1:14)

For he shall give his angels charge over thee, to keep thee in all thy ways. (Psalm 91:11)

Be not forgetful to entertain strangers: for thereby some have entertained angels unawares. (Hebrew 13:2)

It was God's love that saw me through.

The Lord is my shepherd; I shall not want.

He maketh me to lie down in green pastures: he leadeth me beside the still waters.

He restoreth my soul: he leadeth me in the paths of righteousness for his name's sake.

Yea, though I walk through the valley of the shadow of death, I will fear no evil: for thou art with me; thy rod and thy staff they comfort me.

Thou preparest a table before me in the presence of mine enemies: thou anointest my head with oil; my cup runneth over.

Surely goodness and mercy shall follow me all the days of my life: and I will dwell in the house of the Lord for ever." (Psalm 23)

2 Peter 3:8-9

But, beloved, be not ignorant of this one thing, that one day *is* with the Lord as a thousand years, and a thousand years as one day. The Lord is not slack concerning his promise, as some men count slackness; but is longsuffering to us-ward, not willing that any should perish, but that all should come to repentance.

Galatians 6:1-10

Brothers and sisters, if someone is caught in a sin, you who live by the Spirit should restore that person gently. But watch yourselves, or you also may be tempted. 2 Carry each other's burdens, and in this way you will fulfill the law of Christ. 3 If anyone thinks they are something when they are not, they deceive themselves. 4 Each one should test their own actions. Then they can take pride in themselves alone, without comparing themselves to someone else, 5 for each one should carry their own load. 6 Nevertheless, the one who receives instruction in the word should share all good things with their instructor.

John 1:17

For the law was given by Moses, *but* grace and truth came by Jesus Christ.

About the Author

THOMAS L. DOBBINS is a born-again child of God. He was born in 1963 in Centreville, Alabama, to John B. Dobbins and Clara L. Dobbins. He was rebirthed by spirit and water in April 2023.

Thomas is a deacon at Living Faith Outreach Worship Center in Chicago, Illinois. He is also a dad of four beautiful children: Thomas J. Dobbins (Cassandra Allen), Matthew E. Dobbins (Jackie E. Hatcher), Latricia K. Dobbins (Irene Vance), and Rasha J. Hardwick (Juanita Hardwick).